# What She Taught Me, *Too*

Navigating the Joys, Struggles, and Growth of Becoming a Father.

J.L. Ford

Copyright © 2025 by J.L. Ford

All rights reserved. No part of this book may be used or reproduced by any means, graphic, electronic, or mechanical, including photocopying, recording, taping, or by any information storage retrieval system, without the written permission of the publisher except in the case of brief quotations embodied in critical articles and reviews.

# Contents

Preface ........................................................................................... 1

Chapter 1: Shitty Diapers ............................................................. 5

Chapter 2: A Broken Man .......................................................... 11

Chapter 3: This Could Cost You Your Relationship ............... 15

Chapter 4: The Dance of Communication .............................. 34

Chapter 5: The Crying ................................................................ 47

Chapter 6: The Little Things ..................................................... 57

Chapter 7: Triggers ..................................................................... 64

Chapter 8: Protecting the Feminine Energy ............................ 71

Chapter 9: Closer, or Further? ................................................... 79

Chapter 10: They Are What They Are Supposed to Be .......... 89

Chapter 11: Your Values Are Your Responsibility .................. 95

Chapter 12: Peeping Out of the Window .............................. 107

Chapter 13: Everything Is Changing ...................................... 122

Chapter 14: The Perfect Moment ............................................ 128

Afterword shorts ....................................................................... 135

About the Author ..................................................................... 158

# Preface

As I place the final touches on these pages, it dawns on me that it has been about five years since I wrote the very first words of this book. I never intended for it to take this long, but everything seems to take a bit longer when a child enters the picture. Everything. Suddenly, days stretch into months, and months blur into years. I've never been one to move slowly; when I set my sights on something, it's usually pedal to the floor until it's done. But for this book, I was forced to slow down. Perhaps for the best, as it became apparent what I wanted to capture couldn't be rushed.

The moment that pregnancy test read positive, I had a feeling I was in for the ride of my life. I knew the road ahead would be filled with moments that might not feel good when I was in them—moments that would push me to my limits, test my patience, and stretch the very fabric of who I thought I was. But I also knew that stories and lessons worth sharing would be buried in the chaos and sleepless nights, especially for those walking the same path. My god, was I right. This journey has been every bit the blessing I imagined, but it has also been the most challenging experience I have ever encountered.

I wrote this book because I know I'm not alone. There's no shortage of parents who find themselves filled with joy and wonder on day one, only to feel lost and overwhelmed in the following days. Many of us quickly discover that parenting isn't just about raising a child; it's also about maintaining our sanity, navigating our relationships, and finding ourselves in the process. The struggle is real for those of us trying to keep a relationship alive while enduring the demands of new parenting. The love and joy coexist with moments of loss and despair, often more intimately than we ever imagined.

When I began writing, I intended for this book to speak to both parents—to capture the shared experience of raising a child while balancing the weight of a partnership. I have left the essence of that in these pages. But as I reflected on my own journey, I realized that much of what I was experiencing was unique to fathers. So, I decided to focus on the often-unseen struggles of men—the fathers who love deeply, fear silently, and grind through the tough moments with little more than a weary nod and a clenched jaw. This book is a follow-up to my first, *What She Taught Me*, which delved into a man's journey of understanding his masculinity while exploring and connecting with the feminine. If there's one thing I've learned between that book and this one, it's that the practice of growth is far more challenging than the mere knowledge of it. This truth, I hope, is something you'll hold close as you turn these pages.

The goal here isn't perfection—not as a parent, not as a partner, and not as a person. The goal is to understand that everything you experience on this journey is there to serve as a mirror, reflecting who you are in this moment. And the gift of that reflection is the opportunity it offers you: a chance to continuously create and uncover better versions of yourself.

Parenting is not a static role; it's an evolution. It's messy and beautiful, exhausting and exhilarating, all at once. As fathers, we are often handed a narrative of strength and stoicism, but the truth is that we are as vulnerable and raw in this journey as anyone else. In fact, it is in our willingness to confront this vulnerability that we find the real strength—the strength to grow, adapt, and love more deeply than we ever thought possible.

This book is an invitation to embrace that evolution, to lean into the discomfort, to laugh at the absurdities, and to find peace in the chaos. It is a call to all fathers to see themselves not just as providers or protectors but as learners—students in the art of becoming the men and fathers our children need us to be.

So, as you read these pages, I hope you find solace in knowing that you're not alone in this wild, unpredictable, sometimes maddening journey. We're all in it together, figuring it out one day, one moment, one breath at a time.

**To Dahlia,**

I hope that you get to read this book someday; it would be such an honor for me to witness that. I want you to know that you are perfect. I also want you to know that I am always striving to be the father you deserve. I have fallen short so many times, but believe me, it is a goal that I will never stop striving to reach. We've put each other through a lot in these first five years of your life, but it's been beyond amazing and has opened me to parts of myself I could never have seen without you. It's a shame that so little of it will be remembered by you, if any at all. But take my word for it. It has been a ride. Whether this book sells a million copies or none, it will always be the one I am most proud of because it involves you, my real-life princess.

Just do me one favor, beloved: hold on to your ability to turn anything into play, and don't shy away from giving your full self to the world. After all, that is what you came here to do.

With all my love,

Dad

P.S. *You Knucklehead*

# CHAPTER 1
# Shitty Diapers

*"Babies are always more trouble than you thought—and more wonderful."*

**– Charles Osgood**

I started this book at the exact moment I knew I had to write it. It was one of those moments that stops you in your tracks—a moment that involves dishwashing gloves, a tub full of dirty diapers, and me staring at my reflection in the mirror, wondering, "What the hell have I gotten myself into?" Not just a casual thought but a visceral, bone-deep question that seemed to echo around the small, cluttered bathroom.

It felt surreal, like I was looking at a stranger—a version of me that I barely recognized. The face in the mirror was a hollow shell of the person I was just a year ago. I looked worn, like life had aged me beyond my years. My eyes were tired, and there were lines on my face that hadn't been there before. I felt even worse than I looked. And why wouldn't I? I was running on the fumes of broken sleep, mentally and emotionally drained, grasping at the threads of my sanity while chasing after a toddler who seemed to have boundless energy. I was also trying to be a supportive partner while desperately holding together the fragile structure that our entire livelihood depended on. This wasn't the life I had envisioned when I was busy dreaming up a family. It was something else entirely—something I did not feel that I was prepared for or necessarily wanted.

My friends at work could tell you how I used to parade from office to office, spinning tales of my grand quest to find the perfect mother for my future child. It was a lighthearted adventure back then—an exercise in sort of a romantic optimism. They listened, they laughed, and some even tossed in a few nuggets of wisdom about the road ahead. But not one of them, not a single person, warned me about the real journey I was about to embark on. Nobody told me how this journey would strip me down and rebuild me in ways I couldn't have imagined.

No one mentioned that each diaper would become a dollar sign in my mind, calculated as an endless expense every time one was taped into a ball and tossed in the trash. No one prepared me for the fact that babies are born with lungs akin to a semi-truck horn and the stamina of an Olympic swimmer, ready to use both superhuman attributes in the dead of night when you're just slipping into the deepest stage of REM sleep. And definitely, no one told me they'd need their mildly dampened diaper changed precisely at that moment. Maybe this sounds like a bit of venting—and it is. There will probably be more of that throughout these pages. And if you're a parent trying your best, you might find yourself nodding along, maybe even feeling a little relieved that you're not the only one. We'll get into that more later.

These are just a few examples from a long list of harsh nudges that spurred a rude awakening for me. There's something profound that happens when you face yourself in moments like these. It's not just about dealing with a mess in front of you; it's about reckoning with the mess inside you—the parts of yourself that feel lost, overwhelmed, and unsure. In that reflection, I wasn't just seeing a tired father; when I looked in that mirror, I was seeing a man who was grappling with a new reality—a man who was realizing that the journey he thought he was on was entirely different from the one he found himself in.

And honestly, I felt a little betrayed by a society that tends to show only the adorable side of raising little ones. On social media, we're all uploading the best of our worlds while making light of the harder parts, and just about every baby you see on TV or in movies barely cries, or if they do, it's a cute little whimper. It's amazing how, with a gentle bounce and a soft "shhh," they're back to their lines within seconds.

*Not at all, reality.*

I've heard of those mythical, angelic babies, but I'm starting to question those stories along with everything else—like my father's insistence that raising seven kids "wasn't that hard at all" or the constant reminders from well-meaning people that my daughter will be lonely without a sibling. Well, sorry, my little one, you're just going to have to make do with Mommy, Daddy, and whatever friends you can make during Play-Doh time at daycare. As incredible as the parenting journey is, it's a one-and-done situation for me.

And though I'll continue to blame everyone else for my current state of disarray (because it feels good to do so), it's not entirely fair. There was that "Baby Think It Over" program in fifth grade, where I had to care for a crying baby doll for two days straight—I failed. And there was the time I walked into a friend's home to find her and her home completely wrecked by a crawler. I'm sure I just thought it was totally normal because, in my mind, women were superhumans who did this effortlessly—a belief I'm embarrassed to admit I ever held.

So how could I not know that I would end up here, sitting on the rim of a tub filled with the scent of everything I'd fed my child for the past few days? I grew up around little ones. I worked with new families at Head Start schools and even with traumatized ones in the legal system. I taught Human Lifespan as a college psych professor. And still, I didn't see this coming.

I wrestled with this question many times, and two answers emerged. The first, which came to me through my own reflection, was that I'd been shielded from many of the gritty realities of fatherhood because most of the responsibilities traditionally fell on mothers. From what I'd been shown, parenting for fathers was minimal—our burdens were to provide financial stability and deliver discipline when necessary. This freedom allowed me to ignore all the signs and warnings because clearly, they weren't for me. My father's main lesson was to make money and accept that it was all for my family. I accepted that challenge, and that's all I was prepared for.

The other answer, which I find more compelling, is that men don't talk about it. This brings me back to when I realized I needed to write about it. During the throes of the spit-up phase, when I was going through three to four shirt changes a day, I felt like a swollen steam pipe ready to burst. I'm not the type to call up a friend and unload all my complaints, but like many, I'll condense it down to a few sentences and let it out in a social media post. One day, I did just that—shared the horror of keeping up with a toddler and ended with, "What part of parenting is hard for you?" The floodgates opened. I received responses about everything from lack of sleep and financial stress to total burnout and the utter annoyance of whining. Everyone had an answer, and suddenly, I didn't feel so alone.

Then a close male friend commented, "None of it. I love every bit of it…" and continued in a way that made it painfully clear he was overcompensating. Does anybody actually love being startled awake by the sound of a crying baby several times a night? Does anyone enjoy reaching down to hug their child only to accidentally slip their fingers in the poop that ran up their back in a blown-out diaper? I doubt it. This wasn't the first time, nor would it be the last, that I received feedback like his. I started to recognize how those responses made me feel— ashamed. When I realized that it was mostly women sharing the hardships of parenting, it became clear that there wasn't much space for men to air their grievances. Not only are our experiences compared to those of women often minimized, but there will always be some guy out there putting on a show and seeking validation to prove they're a good parent.

I searched my memory for instances of men in my life sharing their struggles with fatherhood. I came up empty. There was drinking, abandonment, and physical abuse, but very few words of wisdom. The prevailing attitude was that you just had to be a man about it. Suffer in silence because the last thing anyone wants is to hear a man complaining about doing his job.

I'm writing this because I believe most men don't want to leave their families or engage in behavior that jeopardizes the structures they've built. They don't want to hide in man caves, grow cold toward their partners and children, or die early from stress. We want to enjoy the homes we've built and the families we've created. And as I've learned, that requires navigating transitions that can be grueling. There are so many changes, demands, and expectations. Bending is sometimes acceptable, but breaking? That's often considered weak. Yet, one thing I want you to take from this read is that this belief—a belief so many of us hold—is not true. Breaking is not weak; it is necessary, especially during this process. Breaking is not something to fear or try to escape when faced with it. We should allow breaking because, as I wrote in the first *"What She Taught Me,"* breaking *will* reveal you to yourself.

# CHAPTER 2

# A Broken Man

*"Life breaks all of us, but some of us get stronger in the broken places."*

– **Ernest Hemingway**

While I looked in the mirror that day, I realized I was staring at a broken man. I didn't like what I saw, so I decided to take immediate action to change things, to reclaim at least a fragment of what I had before we celebrated those two lines on the pregnancy test. I went out and bought a Jeep Wrangler—a man's truck. And to be honest, it worked, at least temporarily. The entire drive home, I sat up high in my new truck, arm hanging out the window, feeling the wind in my palm and a surge of testosterone in my blood. It felt like freedom, like masculinity reclaimed—everything I thought I had lost. I brought my partner outside to show off the truck; she loved it. Then I went back into the house, got spit up on by my daughter, and while changing my shirt, I realized I had just added twenty-thousand dollars' worth of stress onto my shoulders. In reality, I hadn't achieved much—I was still a broken man who had earned himself a brand-new fracture.

Before I started the parenting journey, I was convinced I had reached the highest version of myself. I'd shed so much of my boyhood and mastered much of what it meant to be an adult in this complex society. I felt I'd surpassed my father in many ways because of the experiences I allowed myself to encounter that he never would have. I saw myself as an observer of the world, more than a participant in its games—a testament to what I thought was mature intellect and wisdom. But I would come to understand that maturity is easy to exercise in the relationships we imagine; the true challenges arise in the relationships we allow.

I thought I'd brought myself through enough hard times of my own making. I would create a soft life and enjoy it—and for a time, I did. But I found myself bored rather quickly. One afternoon, while looking over the deck of a hilltop Airbnb in Bermuda, I thought, "I need a child." I don't know where the desire came from; it wasn't one I'd ever had before. But a part of me asked for it, and I accepted, completely blind to the fact that I was walking into the biggest test yet—again, of my own creating.

In other words, life had already broken me more times than I could count, and I'd willingly stepped into more than enough situations where breaking was not just possible but inevitable. I told myself that it was time for a break—a break from being broken—and that this would be my gift to myself for the foreseeable future. I couldn't have been more wrong. Stepping into parenthood, I quickly learned there's rarely a moment to catch your breath. If it isn't life pushing you to the edge, it's you pushing yourself, constantly challenging you to find strength in places you never knew existed.

We can't go long without breaking because everything that lives must grow. Consciously, we can choose to stop growing, and it's normal to do so, especially when we're exhausted by the pain that comes with it. But everything that lives must grow, so other parts of ourselves compel us to do so by employing curiosity, loneliness, desire, boredom, or a host of other tactics, the greatest of all, in my opinion, being love.

There's no avoiding it. Like night follows day, the broken version of yourself is always on the horizon, offering an opportunity to birth a better version. I wish I could tell you that being broken by becoming and being a father is a one-time event, but you will find yourself in that position again and again—each time, needed to reach a version of yourself that can find happiness in this new life.

The challenge is to resist the urge to run and instead dive into the brokenness of yourself, to find the pieces that were previously hidden and use the revealed truths to ascend to a higher level of manhood, consciousness, fatherhood, partnership, and selfhood. That moment of realizing you are broken is different for everyone but always painfully obvious. It's so easy to fall into feelings of failure when faced with that reflection—a failure to your child, your partner, or yourself. I've met myself in this place many times, along with a whirlwind of thoughts and emotions—beating myself up for placing myself in this position, wishing for an easy escape that wouldn't blow up my life or hurt those I love, teetering on the edge of accepting that there may be no way to come out of this as a success.

When you find yourself in those moments, what might save you is believing the opposite of what your mind is telling you. Instead of seeing this as a failure, try to see it as proof that you are in the process of becoming something you've never been before. You are an explorer of your own self, and sometimes you'll stumble over rocks along the way. But remember, you can recover, and each time you do, you come back stronger.

To get through it, you need to give yourself the same grace you'd give anyone who is learning and growing. Believe that the version of yourself you want to be isn't just possible—it's within reach. And know this: whenever you feel like you're breaking, it's not the end. It's an invitation to rebuild yourself—better, wiser, and more complete.

# CHAPTER 3

# This Could Cost You Your Relationship

*"The arrival of a child will awaken new selves, new roles, and new responsibilities in a couple, all of which can come at the expense of the intimacy they once shared."*

– **Esther Perel**

There's a scene in my mind that serves as a grave warning, a vivid memory that surfaces whenever my relationship feels like it's on shaky ground. It's a simple scene, really, but one that has stayed with me, etched into my consciousness like a cautionary tale—the setting: a sweltering day in a Florida botanical garden. The temperature is soaring at around 95 degrees, and I'm terribly dehydrated, my senses dulled and distorted by a heavy dose of mushrooms. My arm is draped over the shoulder of my then-pregnant partner, my body limp and near-useless as she guides me back to the car. I'm struggling to focus, my vision swimming, but I manage to glance back and see her mother in the distance, hurriedly trying to catch up to us.

"Your mother…" I manage to mumble, my tongue heavy in my mouth. Without missing a beat, she replies, "Forget her; I have to make sure you're okay."

The security in those words hits me like a wave, immediate and enveloping. In that instant, I feel more cared for and protected than ever in any relationship. She is here, present, and choosing me above all else—even her own mother. The realization is like a drug; it courses through me, warm and reassuring. I must be important to her, I think. Really important if she is willing to set aside her own mother to make sure I'm alright.

But as quickly as that feeling of safety washes over me, it shifts, darkens, and transforms into something else entirely: dread. A nagging discomfort settles in my chest, and my mind, still spinning from dehydration and psychedelics, makes a startling connection. I gaze back to her mother, who is now just a blur of movement in the hazy distance. What I see isn't just the small, aging figure with bright eyes that I've come to recognize; it's something more profound.

Suddenly, I see the woman who was once inseparably close to her, the one with whom my partner had once been physically one. I see the woman who almost died bringing her into this world, whose body had been both refuge and battlefield in those traumatic moments of birth. Her father once told me how her mother would pace the floor at night, tears streaming down her face, holding her baby daughter close, desperate to comfort her, to stop her cries. That woman, who comforted her through the rawest moments of early life, who fed her, loved her, and watched over her—is now being dismissed. "Forget her," she says.

And in that moment, my perception shifts again. I am no longer just a man being supported by his loving partner. I am now the embodiment of the wedge that has driven a distance between them—a new center of her universe that she has chosen over the one who was there first. The realization sends a chill down my spine, even in the blistering Florida heat. I feel it settling in—a truth I had somehow overlooked in all my naive idealism.

That was the moment I realized I had willed into existence, not just a child, but also as the greatest threat to the very relationship I had sought since my teenage years. For most of my life, I had no desire to have children. I had always thought the idea was ridiculous, something for other people to inflict upon themselves. "Why would anyone want to do that?" I would ask. "Why attach yourself to an expensive ball and chain that sucks the life out of you day and night? It's the most neurotic thing you could do to yourself." Back then, I was certain I was right and steadfast in my beliefs.

But then, something happened—I fell under a spell. I found myself caught in a moment where all those rationalizations and carefully laid beliefs about the dangers and burdens of parenthood started to unravel. Love, desire, the intoxicating idea of family—all these things wove themselves into a powerful enchantment that I didn't see coming.

And now, here I am, in this botanical garden under the unforgiving sun, coming to terms with what I've set in motion. Not just a new life but a reshaping of all the dynamics I thought I understood. A stark realization that in bringing a child into the world, I have also invited in a storm—a force that can transform bonds, twist priorities, and reconfigure the meaning of love and loyalty in ways I never imagined.

### *Life's spells*
I will return to that story, but first, a word about life's spells.

We are all characters living our own stories within a vast, interconnected narrative. In our individual stories, we are the protagonists, and every other character who crosses our path does so to aid our character development. Everything we perceive as happening to us is indeed, in a sense, happening for us. We often connect with certain characters and experiences with excitement, expecting them to lead us to joy or fulfillment, only to discover they were setups for hard lessons we weren't prepared for. And then there are those characters and situations we instinctively avoid, sensing the pain and turmoil they may bring from a mile away. Yet, sometimes, despite our best efforts to steer clear, we have little choice in the matter. We are drawn into the lesson, willing or not.

Life has lessons for all of us, and it's strange, mysterious alchemy has a way of pulling us toward the places where those lessons must be learned. Some of these forces come from deep within—from hidden parts of ourselves that demand attention, compelling us to act in ways that leave us no choice but to face them. This is how I found myself journeying from a firm "never children stance" to being adamant about bringing my little girl into this side of reality.

A divorce was the catalyst that set me adrift, followed by a whirlwind of psychedelic experiences that cracked open my understanding of myself and the world around me. Suddenly, dramatic changes were not only possible but necessary. My thinking about having a child shifted in ways I hadn't anticipated. Even then, I wasn't ready to dive into the deep end of parenthood. I wasn't prepared for the migraine of being a full-time parent, so I devised a plan: I would find someone to co-parent with. I could have my baby and maintain my autonomy—a perfect, balanced equation, or so I thought.

For a year, I dated with that precise intent, but as I passed on one potential partner after another, I began to see more of myself in the process. I discovered parts of me that I had overlooked—parts that longed for me to be more hands-on and involved with than I had ever imagined. Turns out, a child isn't just a source of profound reflection; the very journey of bringing one into the world is a mirror that reflects so many of the hidden facets of who we are. When I finally met the mother of my child, love swept me into the air. And as is often the case with love, it felt exhilarating and full of promise.

But the real work begins after the dust of that sweeping settles. I've come to think of a home as a set, like that of a sitcom—an intimate stage where our stories unfold in real-time. In this set, we see just how much of our parents we carry within us. We may even find ourselves inadvertently reliving their stories, repeating cycles we thought we had escaped. We wake up and fall asleep beside the person who witnesses more of us than anyone else ever will. Here, in this shared space, we are tested emotionally, mentally, and spiritually, revealing where we truly stand in our emotional development, our maturity in relating to another, and the buried pains and traumas we thought were either too deep to resurface or never realized existed. And to make sure we don't throw in the towel just when the journey gets tough, we bring a child home—a bundle of pure magic wrapped in a blanket, a miracle that also serves as an anchor, grounding us to the set when we most want to drift away.

That's how it happened. That's how you ended up where you are. The intoxicating aroma of love (or desire) lifted you off your feet. It carried you, as if weightless, to the crib of your crying child, to the very brink of your sanity, and to the terrifying possibility of losing the relationship you once believed was forever. And maybe what you have standing there now isn't love at all; maybe it's a sense of obligation, fear, or an unexplored part of yourself that longed for this experience, that whispered this was the path you need to walk. No matter what the spell was made of, the essence of this journey isn't about what drew you in but about the lesson waiting to be learned. That lesson is the cornerstone of everything: your future, your relationship with your child, and your relationship with your partner depend on it.

That was where the dread came from that day—the weight of the realization that being a good partner was no longer enough to sustain the love I had always longed for. I would also have to figure out how to be good at something I had no experience in: a good parent to the child we created together. And not just "good" by my standards, but by the standards of the one who was carrying her. I would have to confront all the unspoken expectations, the silent judgments, and the deep-seated fears of failing at this most sacred role.

It is here, in this space of uncertainty and challenge, that true growth happens. We must grapple with our own limitations and stretch beyond them, learn to balance our needs with the needs of another, and discover that love isn't just a feeling but an active, living practice. And this is the heart of the story we are all writing—a story that is both intensely personal and universally human, a journey that shapes not only who we are but who we are becoming.

## *Nostalgia*

Another moment often comes to mind—a moment that seems frozen in time, like a photograph with the edges soft and worn from constant handling. It was before the child, before the sleepless nights and endless routines, back when the world was just the two of us lying in bed in the middle of the day. We may have been slightly high, floating between reality and a gentle dream. My head nestled perfectly in the small of her back as she doodled on a sketchpad, lost in her own creative world. I snapped pictures of us—trying to capture the essence of that moment, its lightness, its simplicity, its quiet perfection. I remember whispering to her, "I want nothing to change. I want to live here, in this moment, forever." And then, as life always does, everything changed.

That memory is a bittersweet reminder—a snapshot of a time untouched by the weight of what was to come. It is so easy to get caught up in what was before, to long for the days when life felt simpler and freer, when love felt like a constant, unburdened by the pressures of parenting and the relentless march of time. But holding on too tightly to what once was can become a trap, pulling us away from the present and into a place of resentment, regret, or even depression. The longing for what has passed can distract us from what is, from the richness and complexity of the now—this moment that, whether we realize it or not, is what we will someday yearn for, too.

We've all experienced it—an older person looking at our children with a wistful smile, a distant look in their eyes. They tell us how much they miss these days, imploring us with all the wisdom of hindsight to "enjoy the journey because it's over before you know it." Sometimes, it feels like just another cliché, another platitude meant to comfort or inspire. But beneath those words is a profound truth. Time slips away so quietly, almost imperceptibly, until you wake up one day, and the world you knew has completely transformed into something else. The moments that seemed mundane or exhausting—the sleepless nights, the chaotic mornings, the messes, the endless questions—are the very moments we will come to miss.

So, what do we do with this knowledge? How do we balance the ache for what was with the weight of what is without losing ourselves in either? The answer, I think, is not just to survive but to actively choose to enjoy—to savor the journey, however messy or challenging it may be. It's about finding the beauty in the chaos, the magic in the mundane, and the connection in the chaos of everyday life.

The truth is the present moment is all we ever really have. It's the only place where life unfolds, love is expressed, lessons are learned, and growth truly happens. And just like that moment from before—the one where I wanted nothing to change—we must learn to love what is in front of us, even as it changes because it will change and be over before we know it.

There is something sacred in that understanding, a call to live with eyes wide open, fully engaged in the here and now. To see each day not just as another day to get through but as another opportunity to create new memories, to learn more about ourselves and each other, and to write the next chapter in our unfolding stories. Life is never static; it is always in motion, always evolving. And while we may not be able to live in any moment forever, we can carry the essence of those moments with us, learning to weave the past, the present, and the future into a richer, more meaningful tapestry of experience.

Because, in the end, that is what life is—a series of moments that, strung together, tell the story of who we are and who we are becoming. It's up to us to ensure that this story is not just one of endurance but of joy, love, and a deep, abiding presence.

A few things to note on this journey: **You are responsible**. Not just for a great deal of your child's life experience but also for your own experience as a parent and partner. It's easy to forget that, amidst the chaos and unpredictability, we hold immense power over how we perceive and respond to the moments that make up our lives. Two parents could face the same scenario—an uncooperative child, a sudden change in plans, or a moment of feeling lost and overwhelmed—yet experience it completely differently. What that means for you is that it's entirely possible to experience it differently, too, in a way that aligns more closely with who you want to be and how you want to live.

You don't have to allow yourself to remain upset when your child is being rebellious; instead, you can choose to approach the situation with understanding. Perhaps this rebellion is a cry for independence, a test of boundaries, or a simple expression of frustration. What if you saw it as an opportunity to connect, teach, and grow together rather than as a battle to be won? You don't have to let frustration thrive when things don't go as planned; you can laugh at the absurdity of life and find a moment of levity in the chaos. After all, plans are only frameworks, and life loves to color outside the lines. You don't have to feel like a bad parent when you don't have all the answers; you can approach the unknown with curiosity, viewing each challenge as a chance to learn and expand.

Everything you experience is, in many ways, a reflection of yourself—your thoughts, beliefs, expectations, and capacity for growth. This doesn't mean dismissing or minimizing the difficulties; it means recognizing that within every experience lies the power to shape it, to bend it toward a more compassionate, understanding, and fulfilling narrative. And it is within your power to change what you wish to see changed, starting from within.

One of the most crucial steps in this transformation is **_acceptance_**—the understanding that what was is now no more. So much of the sadness, frustration, or even depression you may experience can stem from an unwillingness to let something go—a time, a feeling, a version of yourself or your life that no longer exists. Ironically, in many cases, what we cling to is no longer there to hold on to; it exists only in the mind, in the stories we tell ourselves about how things used to be and how they "should" have been. It's time to loosen that tight grip on the past and fully embrace your present before that, too, slips away into memory.

Perhaps letting go requires a grieving process, and that's okay. Grief is not something to be rushed or dismissed; it is a natural part of human experience, a way for us to acknowledge the passing of what was and make room for what is and what could be. But let's not forget the other side of the coin: what is life but a continuous stream of experiences where we grieve, suffer, and then heal and grow? It may sound somber but consider this—this cycle of letting go and moving forward is only possible because we also experience the pleasantries of life, the moments of joy, wonder, connection, and love. It is these highs and lows, these cycles of holding on and letting go, that gives life its depth and richness.

To accept this flow is to realize that each moment, no matter how challenging or beautiful, is a passing wave in the ocean of our existence. When we learn to ride these waves rather than resist them, we open ourselves up to the full spectrum of life. We learn that while we may not control the waves themselves, we can choose how we navigate them. We can choose presence over regret, curiosity over judgment, laughter over frustration, and love over fear.

This does not suggest that this journey is easy or without pain. It is to say that it is worth it. It is worth the effort of cultivating a new perspective, shedding the layers of old stories that no longer serve us, and embracing the present with open arms and an open heart. In doing so, we reclaim our power as parents or partners and as human beings, constantly evolving, learning, and becoming. We reclaim our right to experience life not as victims of circumstance but as active participants in its unfolding, capable of shaping our reality with every breath, every choice, and every act of love.

So, take a deep breath. Feel the weight of the past begin to lift and the lightness of the present settle in. Know that every step forward is a choice, a small act of courage and faith in the story still being written—the one where you are both the author and the main character, fully present, fully alive.

**Be present and intentional.** As one of my favorite teachers, Ram Dass, would say: *be here now*. The more we anchor ourselves in the present moment, especially in the whirlwind experience of parenthood, the more the journey unfolds with beauty and depth. To be present is to be open, to notice the small moments that often pass us by unnoticed, and to find joy and meaning in them. When you consider the totality of parenting, what comes to mind for you? For me, the first thoughts often revolve around the hardships: the relentless crying and whining, the seemingly endless expenses, the constant calls for my attention, and the non-stop nature of it all—the list goes on. It's easy to get lost in the challenges and to feel overwhelmed by the sheer weight of responsibility.

But then I remember the power of intention—the ability to choose how I think and feel about these experiences. When I shift my focus, I am reminded of the moments that fill my heart: her wonderful smile, those deep belly laughs that come when she says the funniest things, and the moments when her mother and I sit quietly, just watching her with awe, amazed that this little being is here because of a decision we made and a journey we took together. The hardships may remain there, but they no longer dominate the narrative. Instead, they become the backdrop to the beauty, the contrast that makes the joys stand out even more vividly.

***Your fears can serve you well, but they make for terrible masters.*** That's a lesson I've learned from another favorite teacher of mine, Alan Watts. Fears, if allowed to take control, can become self-fulfilling prophecies. They can lead us into the situations we try to avoid, looping us back to the same place repeatedly. Fear, when left unchecked, has a way of tightening its grip, causing us to act in ways that align with the fear rather than with love, understanding, or growth.

Here's a scene that captures this dynamic—a moment that taught me more about presence and intention than I ever could have imagined.

It's a little more than three years after my startling realization at the botanical garden. I'm with my little family, sitting at a charming café on the vibrant streets of Puerto Viejo, Costa Rica. The trip had been long and exhausting, but now I'm looking forward to a quiet, enjoyable breakfast in this colorful, artsy space. My partner is in beautiful spirits, her laughter light and infectious, and our little one, Dahlia, is building towers with blocks while we wait for our food. The air is fresh with a gentle breeze, and the sky is a clear, brilliant blue. The set couldn't be more perfect—a moment that feels like a gift.

Then, the waitress arrives, setting down our plates. A true-to-Costa Rica veggie sandwich for me, omelets for my partner, and a large bowl of brown sugar and cinnamon oatmeal for Dahlia—her absolute favorite. Again, perfect. I test the temperature of the oatmeal and, regretfully, inform our little one that it's too hot and she'll have to wait just a bit. And, of course, this small delay triggers a full meltdown. Suddenly, her wails fill the café, and the idyllic morning begins to crumble. Her mother, holding onto the radiant energy she woke up with—the same energy that once was reserved for our quiet, intimate moments, for my comfort and pleasure—tries to calm her. She gives her everything she has, but it's not enough to break the meltdown. Eventually, she takes Dahlia back to our flat while I wait for the bill.

Before I know it, I'm sitting alone at the table, staring at three untouched plates of what suddenly feels like grossly overpriced food. At that moment, as I listen to the echoes of other people's laughter and conversations, my mind drifts back to the botanical garden, back to the times when it was just us, when everything seemed simpler. Except now, it's me who is being left behind.

These are the moments when fear is most seductive. It whispers narratives of regret, anger, jealousy, and resentment when it creeps in. Fear wants to convince me that I've lost something essential, that my daughter has "taken my partner away from me," and that I am now on the outside looking in. This is when we have to catch ourselves and recognize that we are standing at a crossroads. In these very moments, when we come face to face with what we fear most, our actions will determine whether our fears become our reality or dissolve into nothingness.

There is a part of me that wants to give in, to feel angry at Dahlia for "ruining" a perfect morning, to resent my partner for leaving me alone at the table. But I know, deep down, that this is the path that leads to separation, to the very thing I fear. Instead, I choose differently. I choose to stay present. I take a deep breath, pay the bill, and return to our flat. I find my partner and hug her, feeling the warmth of her presence. I play with my Dahlia, letting her laughter be the melody that fills the room. I didn't get the breakfast I had hoped for, but I end up experiencing the moments I truly needed.

Parenting is a practice, not a performance. It is about showing up, again and again, in love and in struggle, in joy and in frustration. It's about realizing that the messy, imperfect moments are as much a part of the story as the idyllic ones. It's about seeing beauty in the chaos and finding peace amid the noise. And most importantly, it's about understanding that every moment, even the challenging ones, offers an opportunity to connect more deeply—with our children, partners, and ourselves.

So, in those moments of doubt and difficulty, when fear tries to take the wheel, remember that you have a choice. You can choose to let fear drive you apart, or you can choose to move closer, to build bridges rather than walls, and to create the life and relationships you truly desire. Because in the end, it's not about the perfect breakfast or the perfect moment; it's about the love that binds us together through it all.

And that, I've learned, is the real journey—the one worth being present for.

## *Postpartum Depression: The Overlooked Shadow*

When I think of postpartum depression, images and fragments come to mind, all coming together to form a larger picture. These fragments are influenced by the clippings from TV shows and movies that depict women as either unwilling to be around their child or as a danger to themselves and their baby. As someone with experience in treating mental health illnesses, I believed I had a solid idea of what postpartum depression (PPD) would look like. I felt confident that I would recognize it if it appeared in my own life, and I was prepared to be there for my partner in the ways she might need during such a vulnerable time. But when it mattered most, I didn't recognize it, and I wasn't there for her in the way I now wish I could have been. It took a toll on our relationship, and it lingers even now.

How did that happen? Well, that picture I had in my mind of postpartum depression didn't match what I saw every day in the relationship between my daughter and her mother. She showed our daughter a level of tenderness and love that I had longed for as a child and that I desperately wanted for her. She was attentive, gentle, and deeply caring—sometimes to the point where I felt pangs of jealousy. There were many moments when she was with our child, and I would just watch, longing for the time when I had all her attention. We had our share of debates over what was best for our daughter, and her mind was unwaveringly focused on ensuring our child felt heard, loved, understood, respected, safe, and comfortable. She embodied the role of a mother in every sense of the word, so the thought of postpartum depression never crossed my mind. It didn't occur to me that it could be why I felt so alone in shouldering the weight of parenting.

I had come to expect certain things from her—things she brought into our relationship that inspired me to take this journey together. I used to come home to a house that wasn't just clean; her energy illuminated it. She filled every corner with light and warmth, making it feel like home. Her enthusiasm was infectious—there was always some new dish she had experimented with, waiting for me to try, and her laughter filled the space, creating an atmosphere that felt like the best kind of magic. It was an amazing period in our relationship, a reality I would have traded anything for. But in the midst of raising a newborn, much of what I loved about the early days of our relationship seemed to drift away, like they were taken by a gentle wave retreating into a vast sea of memories.

The once vibrant home now felt dim and disorganized. The exciting meals we once shared were replaced by hastily prepared, unremarkable dishes. Her once-bounding energy for life seemed to have been replaced by a heavy stillness, like a weight pressing down on her shoulders. The worst times were the mornings. I'd often wake up early, alone with our daughter, my body tense with anticipation as I rushed to her room, hoping to catch her before she smeared the contents of her diaper on the walls or floor. My partner's lowest depressive moments coincided with a phase where our daughter developed an uncanny fascination with the stinky brown substance that inevitably forced its way out of her small body. If I didn't get there in time, I knew I was destined for a chaotic, messy start to an already long day.

Each morning, I woke up on high alert, leaving my partner in bed while I braced myself for whatever awaited me in Dahlia's room. The air was thick with silence as I tiptoed down the hall, feeling the heaviness of the quiet house around me. Most mornings, I was too late to avert disaster. I'd find myself wiping, vacuuming, spraying, and scrubbing the room—and my daughter—before moving on to the next few hours of overstimulation with a hyperactive toddler alone. The mornings felt like an obstacle course of small, relentless challenges, each one pulling at my patience.

As every morning minute passed, my anxiety would grow, tightening like a vice around my chest while anger simmered beneath the surface. My thoughts raced, swirling with bitterness and resentment. I couldn't help but think about how, while I struggled, my partner slept peacefully upstairs, untouched by the chaos. When she finally came downstairs, bursting into the room with energy like Kramer from *Seinfeld*, I was so resentful that my face would harden, and I'd greet her with a cold, bitter look that conveyed everything I was feeling. Most days, we wouldn't even share a touch before I walked out the door, leaving her the way I felt she had left me—alone. I needed the space to feel like I could breathe, even if that meant turning my back on the reality we were both living. I convinced myself that she simply didn't care, and to survive, I thought I needed to care less, too, at least for a few hours each day.

Our relationship hovered in this vulnerable space for some time. The only thing that seemed to hold us together was our shared commitment to always be there for our daughter when, in reality, better communication should have been our focus. We were like two islands, close yet separate, connected only by our devotion to our child while drifting further apart from each other.

We had countless arguments during this period and just as many conversations after the storm had passed. But it wasn't until recently that she opened up and revealed the truth: during those mornings when I thought she was blissfully dreaming, she was actually lying there, wide awake, paralyzed by a wave of depression so deep it made getting out of bed feel impossible. She admitted there were moments when she didn't know how to make it through another day. When I heard that, it felt like a punch to the gut. All this time, I thought she had left me alone to manage the chaos of co-parenting, but in truth, I had left her alone, battling a darkness I never recognized.

I had no idea she was fighting that battle in silence, and though I know she has forgiven me, I will carry that burden with me for the rest of my life. Knowing that, when she needed me most, I wasn't there is a burden that sits heavy in my heart.

What I've learned from this experience is that postpartum depression isn't always obvious. It doesn't always resemble the extreme depictions we see in movies or TV. It can be subtle, creeping in like a shadow, manifesting in inconspicuous ways that it's easy to mistake it for something else—something that breeds resentment and anger instead of the care and empathy that are truly needed. We made it through, but I know many couples do not. The high rate of separation and divorce within the first year of having a child is often linked to these unseen, unspoken struggles.

Make education on postpartum depression a priority. Familiarize yourself not only with the symptoms of PPD but also with what you'll need to do as a couple to navigate it together. Equip yourself with the knowledge and tools necessary to support one another so that, when you reach the other side of that journey, you can look back and feel proud of how you stood by each other during one of the most vulnerable periods of your relationship.

# CHAPTER 4

# The Dance of Communication

*"The first duty of love is to listen."*

– Paul Tillich

The dances that captivate us most are those marked by elegance and grace—movements flowing with seamless fluidity that draw us in and hold us spellbound. There's something about the uninterrupted flow of moving energies, whether in the passionate whirlwind of Salsa, the disciplined poise of Ballet, or the electrifying spontaneity of contemporary dance, which causes us to marvel in awe. But let us not limit ourselves to these images alone; we are entranced by the dance in all forms—sports with their fluid plays and dynamic coordination, the rhythm of spoken word poetry, the harmonies of music, the intimate dance of lovemaking, and even the mesmerizing cycles of nature. There is a sweetness in witnessing a dance that moves in such perfect flow, a sense of magic in its rarity, perhaps because it mirrors the rare moments of perfect alignment in our own lives.

For often, we encounter dances interrupted by missteps, misunderstandings, unexpected pauses, and changes in rhythm—impediments that can feel like stumbles on our path to grace. These interruptions, while natural and perfect in their own right, are rarely as delightful to watch, let alone experience.

They are the moments when we realize that what we often perceive as failure or imperfection is simply another aspect of the dance—one that calls for patience, awareness, and growth.

So, how do we reach the point where the dance feels so fluid and effortless that it becomes an art form unto itself? Because it never starts that way. The pianist begins with fingers that fumble over keys, just as the gymnast falls again and again before mastering even the most basic flips. The fluidity we admire in any art form or practice comes only after a long journey of dedication, perseverance, and countless repetitions of getting it wrong. Their paths to fluidity are filled with other dances—dances within the dance. They must first learn how to learn, how to train, and how to attune themselves to the subtle nuances of movement, rhythm, and balance. Only then do they achieve a state where the dance becomes second nature, allowing the audience to feel the deep emotion and artistry that flows from every movement.

This journey to fluidity reminds me of savoring a favorite dish, like Bermuda's fish chowder. At first bite, I am transported—sitting back in my seat, closing my eyes, and allowing myself to be fully present with the magic of the flavors. I know little about the intricate process that goes into making it, but I do know that when the preparation—the dance—is done right, the experience is nothing short of spiritual. The flavors are harmonious, each element complementing the others in an intentional and effortless way. But this harmony is only possible because of the labor and love that goes into it, the precise attention to detail that makes the final dish a masterpiece.

This should be and can be, the taste of your relationship—the dance with the feminine or any partner who holds your heart.

In the beginning, this is exactly what we get to savor in relationships. Everything is so fresh, so new, and so uncomplicated that the energies easily connect and flow. The excitement of discovery, the joy of learning each other's rhythms, and the beauty of the unknown create a sense of magic and ease. But as time passes, we begin to see what is attached to that energy—the layers of personality, beliefs, values, past wounds, fears, and expectations. While beautiful in their own right, these complexities often appear as impediments to connection, creating distance where there was once only closeness. This is where the real dance begins—*the dance of communication.*

We've all heard that "communication is the key to a healthy relationship." It sounds cliché, but it holds profound truth. Communication is the tool we use to navigate the obstacles that block our path to deeper connection. The key opens doors to understanding, compassion, partnership, and all the other elements necessary for dancing fluidly together. Without it, we are left fumbling in the dark, stepping on each other's toes, and falling out of sync. But even with the best intentions, fluid communication is rare. The impediments are countless. Many of us have found ourselves moving beautifully to the rhythm of connection, only to stumble on the judgment of a partner, a flare of anger, a dismissive attitude, or the invalidation of feelings. And if we are honest with ourselves, we must admit that we have all been guilty of more than a few of these missteps.

Anything that disrupts fluid communication is an obstacle that keeps us from the ultimate goal: deeper connection.

But here's the deeper truth: whatever the obstacle is, it may be more significant than the specific issue you're trying to communicate about and even the relationship with your partner itself. That's because every obstacle points back to something within. Each misstep in the dance is an invitation to look inward, to examine where and why one might be holding tension, fear, or unresolved pain. It is an opportunity to ask yourself, "What am I protecting? What am I afraid of losing? What part of me needs healing?"

Before meeting my partner, I considered myself an excellent communicator. Years of working as a therapist had trained me to listen deeply, to ask the right questions, and to help people see parts of themselves that they either couldn't or wouldn't see. I believed I could bring these skills into my romantic relationship seamlessly. But the dance is different when you're moving with a romantic partner because so much more is on the line—it's personal. There is vulnerability in being truly seen, which comes with the risk of rejection, misunderstanding, and hurt. When you're just learning each other, it's easy to step on each other's toes, to misinterpret intentions, and to react defensively.

Let me share an example from my own journey—a struggle with communication in my current partnership that taught me more about myself than I ever expected. I pride myself on being a great partner, so when my partner shares experiences of me that don't align with that image—experiences where she felt hurt, unseen, or misunderstood—I tend to take it hard. As she speaks—softly and thoughtfully—I can feel a burning sensation in my chest and muscles tightening. My thoughts begin to race with anger and defensive arguments, and it shows on my face as my eyes squint and brows furrow. Before she even finishes, I interrupt with my defenses, eager to rewrite the "wrong" story in her mind. And just like that, she shuts down—perhaps a misstep of her own in response to mine.

In those moments, I feel it when she closes off, and I know my mistake caused this abrupt end to the dance within the dance. Because of that misstep, we fail to navigate the issue at hand, and instead of growing closer, we drift a little farther apart. I may have defended my image of myself, but in doing so, I lost a bit of the connection with the feminine who holds my heart. This is why the impediment is just as important as the fluidity of the dance. It allows you to see the parts of yourself that need your attention. It allows you to bring healing, understanding, and compassion to those parts of you that are hurting or reactive.

Your partner is more than just your love; your partner is your mirror. In those moments, there is a reflection that needs your care and awareness. I could focus on defending myself when my partner offers her criticisms, or I could simply listen to her words and my body, which is trying to communicate with me through those strong physical reactions. No matter how much I try to be receptive to her until I move past that defensive part of myself, I won't be able to truly hear her and dance toward a higher level of connection.

### *Your relationship with yourself is your most important relationship.*

Once more, your partner is your mirror. Many people choose a distorted mirror—a partner who reflects only what makes them feel good about themselves. If "ignorance is bliss" were a relationship, that would be it. However, ignorance often comes at a higher cost than the supposed peace of mind it provides, whether or not the person who purchases it ever truly realizes this.

When you find the one you truly belong with, you will also find the clearest mirror. As long as you stand in front of a mirror that reflects your perfectly imperfect self, you commit to a challenging journey of self-discovery and growth. And it is within this journey that you must learn how to dance. This dance includes the most important conversations you can have—the ones within your own mind. The dance also involves the labor of repairing the broken parts of yourself. For the dance to be fluid, it requires thinking about and regulating your thoughts, allowing your emotions and feelings to pass through you, and having compassion for yourself, much like a mother has for her child. Think of a time when you had a wound or sore spot on your physical body; whenever someone moved too close to that area, you would instinctively jerk away to protect it. This is no different from what we do when the sore spots of our emotional bodies are at risk of further injury. We don't think about it; it's a natural reflex to protect ourselves. But when dancing with a partner who truly cares about your well-being and the health of your connection, defending yourself shouldn't be necessary because you are a team with the shared goal of deepening that connection.

This brings to mind a saying I'm sure you've heard before: "I don't want to step on anyone's toes." People say this to indicate that the goal of the next steps in this communication dance is to elevate the relationship, not to cause offense or pain. But toes will always be stepped on, vulnerable areas will always be made sore by touch, and an upset partner will always bring the dance to a halt. All of this is okay. You and your partner should have the space to feel, pause, and take a break from the dance if necessary. But what you do not have to do is fight each other. When you're a team with the same goal in mind, you find a way to address the internal or external impediment so that you can return to the dance floor and move together until the next challenge arises.

The dance of relationships is not about avoiding missteps or pretending the dance will always be flawless. It's about recognizing the beauty in the imperfect steps, the grace that comes from learning together, and the strength that emerges when two people are committed to understanding and growing. It is about the continual practice of aligning your movements, holding space for each other's growth, and choosing to dance again and again, no matter how many times you stumble. This is the dance of true intimacy, of real connection, and of lasting love.

To dance well with another, we must first learn to dance well with ourselves. This means being willing to explore our own minds and hearts, confront our fears and insecurities, and cultivate a deep sense of compassion and curiosity about who we are. It means learning to recognize when we are out of sync with ourselves and taking the time to realign, to ground ourselves in our own truth so that we can move with more intention and grace. Only then can we show up fully for the dance with our partner.

In a relationship, the dance never truly ends. There will always be new rhythms to learn, new steps to master, and new ways to grow together. There will be moments of pure harmony, where everything flows effortlessly, and there will be moments of discord, where nothing seems to fit. But if we can remember that every step, every stumble, and every pause is part of the dance, we can find joy in the journey. We can learn to appreciate the dance not for its perfection but for its authenticity—for the way it allows us to be fully human, fully alive, and fully in love.

And so, we dance. We dance through the laughter and the tears, the joy and the pain, the moments of clarity and the moments of confusion. We dance because it is through the dance that we come to know ourselves and each other more deeply. We dance because it is in the movement, in the rhythm of connection, that we find the true essence of love.

## *A child in the middle*

I emphasize the importance of learning the dance of communication and continually fine-tuning it because when a child arrives, that dance can feel nearly impossible. Looking back, I deeply wish we had taken the time to perfect our rhythm before our baby was born. I was too eager, too caught up in the excitement of becoming parents, to focus on the groundwork our relationship needed. I imagine that had we devoted ourselves to mastering this delicate dance of connection; it would have made those first exhausting years smoother. Trying to reach my partner on a deeper level often felt like shouting across a chasm with a baby between us, muffling the words and intentions we needed to share.

With a young child around, even the smallest conversation becomes a luxury. It's as if she has a radar; when we sit down to talk, she suddenly finds a thousand reasons to interject, even if she had been perfectly content on her own a moment before. When we embrace, she races over, crawling between our legs as if she's squeezing under a bridge, demanding to be part of this closeness that feels like play but, for us, is a precious and fleeting attempt to reconnect. Thinking of these moments now fills me with an endearing nostalgia, but their reality often brings stress and frustration. There's an ache in feeling that, even in those brief, stolen moments, I can't quite reach the woman I love. And it's in these small, missed connections that cracks can begin to form in a relationship. Too much time is spent, unable to truly connect, and partners slowly drift apart.

That's why I urge anyone anticipating the arrival of a child to make communication and connection a priority before they arrive—and to keep them a priority after. Reserve the time and space, even when it feels inconvenient, to nurture the bond that brought you together in the first place. Achieving a state of fluidity in this dance, one that adapts as you shift from partners to parents will ultimately strengthen the family as a whole. This commitment to connection, not just to the child but to each other, becomes the foundation on which the family stands.

### *Some advice on conflict resolution*

**A conflict doesn't always have to be a fight.** Raising a child with someone will present many opportunities for conflict, which can lead to fights. However, it can also lead to growth and a deeper connection. When you find yourselves in a moment where a disagreement or conflict about parenting styles arises, remember these four pieces of advice:

1. **Resolution Can Often Wait.** Sometimes, working out issues in front of your children is beneficial. When your

communication is healthy and constructive, it can serve as a valuable lesson for them on how to navigate conflicts effectively. However, most times, it's best to wait. When tensions are slightly higher, egos can be fragile, trigger more sensitivity, and active listening is more challenging. Navigating these conversations can be difficult enough without these obstacles—not to mention the constant interruptions of a child seeking attention every few seconds.

2. **Immediate Change Isn't Always Necessary**. If you reach a resolution in the moment, remember that immediate change isn't required. As I've pointed out, you will learn about yourself as a parent as you journey through this experience. You will encounter situations you've never faced, which may prompt an instinctual response. Sometimes, it's better to pause before acting. If the situation is new to you, ensure that your response aligns with how you'll feel about it in the future. This approach is far more effective than making a change that leads to regret. Reflecting on this reminds me of when I snatched an Oreo from my daughter's mouth just before she could savor its delicious crunch. Her aunt had just given it to her, and I lunged to take it away like Dennis Rodman going after a loose ball. That moment forced me to confront my own issues with food and my controlling tendencies. Dahlia burst into tears; I felt terrible, and her aunt likely did too. That moment could have waited. Dahlia could have enjoyed her cookie, but instead, she experienced her dad's unresolved trauma around food. Children, especially

when enjoying something, aren't fans of sudden changes. Often, necessary changes can be delayed a bit to avoid unnecessary outbursts or tantrums.

3. **Remember You Are Doing This Together.** With different parenting styles and diverse opinions on how things should be done, you can easily view your co-parent as an adversary. This mindset is fertile ground for regrettable words and actions, some of which may be hard to heal from. During high-stress periods, remember that you both share the same desire: what is best for the child. When this is true, you can trust that no matter the conflict, the person you chose to have this child with is your partner, not your enemy. If you struggle to find a solution, focus on finding kindness. The solution will always reveal itself from a place of kindness.

4. **Don't Forget to Repair.** If things don't go well, don't neglect to repair. One thing I must admit about the advice in this book is that nearly all of it is easier said than done. Expect to miss the mark at times, even when you know better. There may be moments when you miss the mark so badly that you find yourselves in a heated face-off, wondering how a couple with so much magic between them could end up in such a dark place. There will be times when you act in ways that harm your family—just don't walk away without doing the work of repairing. Moving on without discussing what happened or enduring the emotional labor of making amends can be tempting. But without that repair, wounds remain open or sensitive to the touch. Even if

everyone seems to get along or function in their roles, unresolved issues can create a chasm that prevents genuine and deep connection.

Whatever scenes you are experiencing on your life's stage are all perfect because they present opportunities to grow into better alignment with your higher self—the version of yourself you aspire to be. They allow you to become closer to your partner and experience true intimacy. They are also perfect because they offer the opportunity to dismantle the life you have built, which is sometimes necessary to fully see yourself.

I cannot stress enough that everything you experience, internally and externally, is a mirror. Building your life is also the process of erecting mirrors that reflect certain parts of you. Sometimes, we bring something into our lives and soon after decide to walk away from it for various reasons, like disliking what we see in the reflection or simply not enjoying the experience. But what happens when you're struggling with a part of your life that you can't easily walk away from due to commitment, a sense of duty, responsibility, or love? You can either walk away and lose those parts of your life or look at the reflection and work on what is necessary to keep them.

If you want to hold onto these relationships and give them what they need to thrive, when you find yourself at a crossroads—where you can choose to focus on what divides you or brings you together—always choose the path that brings you together.

A child entering the picture will bring more challenges to your relationship. Responsibilities increase tremendously; there's less time for each other, unexpected differences in parenting styles emerge, financial strains arise, intimacy levels falter, communication becomes more challenging and much more. Previously unknown aspects of you and your partner will surface, causing issues. Trying to navigate these changes will be more difficult, especially with all the crying, whining, feeding, and lack of sleep added to your lives. Nevertheless, love always provides a path to reconnect. You can choose to take it or take the easier paths that lead to watching the connection and your partner fade away.

# CHAPTER 5

# The Crying

*Congratulations, my friend; RIP to sleep for the next 5 years.*

**– A friend of mine upon learning we were expecting.**

Somewhere near the beginning of the second year of my daughter's life, I became convinced that something was terribly wrong with me. I had always been mentally sharp, my mind a steady stream of clear, organized thoughts. But suddenly, that river of ideas had dried up, replaced by a thick, unyielding fog. Short-term memories became more like puzzles I had to solve than things I could simply recall. Words would often escape me, turning conversations into frustrating games of charades, and what were once menial tasks at times felt like chores of Herculean effort. I remember a friend teasing me about possibly being a hypochondriac. There may have been some truth to that in the past, but this time, I was almost certain there was an issue with my brain. "What if it's brain cancer?" I wondered. It seems like everyone is dropping from some kind of cancer these days, so it wasn't far-fetched.

I began a deep dive into self-diagnosis, researching lesions, tumors, and other diseases that could cause nerve damage. I even considered the possibility that I might have suffered ministrokes. I went on quite the journey for a healthy 37-year-old with no family history of any such issues.

Convinced that something was wrong, I underwent a CT scan on my brain. Fortunately, I had support to hold my hand through the excruciating wait—my old friends, anxiety and the feeling of impending doom. When my doctor handed me the results, he said, "You're perfectly fine." With that, anxiety and doom moved over to make room for confusion. Not quite believing him, I stared at the scan, searching for something—because something had to be wrong. The physician asked, "How much sleep have you been getting?"

I paused and considered his question. "Not much," I replied. I hadn't realized just how little "not much" was until I started tracking my sleep. It turned out "not much" amounted to about 2.5 hours per night, with barely any REM. Immediately, I knew what the problem was. Well, not the problem—the symptom. The real problem was the crying. *The goddamn crying.*

**Nobody warned me about the crying.**

Maybe they sort of did back in middle school when I volunteered to carry around a baby doll for a few days as part of the "Baby Think It Over" program. The whole purpose was to make kids think twice about unprotected sex by giving them a taste of the responsibilities of caring for a baby. That experience stung; it did make me "think it over." But in no way could it have prepared me for the real thing. The cry of that doll was an irritant, nothing more. It didn't shake me to my core the way my own child's cries do, nor did it leave me with phantom cries that jolted me out of my dreams in the middle of many nights. The program didn't reveal how the relentless crying could erode the connection between mother and father, how it could spark a deep, irrational anger toward an innocent child, or how it could feel so torturous that one might consider not wanting to be alive anymore, as was the case for me.

This chapter is about how to survive the crying, but first, let's explore why it's so terrible in the first place.

First, it's biology. Your child's cry is designed to shake you to your core, to activate something primal and urgent in you, so you feel almost no choice but to respond immediately. A comprehensive study published in the *Proceedings of the National Academy of Sciences* showed that our brains are hardwired to respond to a baby's cry, heightening activity in the parts of the brain responsible for caregiving, movement, and speech. It goes on to share that mothers would respond within five seconds on average. That's a tremendous demand on the nervous system, especially if you're dealing with a chronic crier. The same study also shares that prolonged crying can trigger feelings of neglect or even thoughts of maltreatment. I can relate to the latter. While I have never acted on it, I have felt anger and resentment toward my child for crying more often than I have felt the instinct to rush to care. I have found that many parents deal with the same feelings internally, working to be the caring, attentive, loving parents they wish to be in those excruciating moments. Many will be reluctant to be honest with themselves about what those cries trigger. But being honest about what is happening internally gives us a foundation of truth to build something better—a better parent for the child we brought into this world. There's my mid-chapter TED Talk.

When your child is ringing your bell with cries from their superhuman lungs, just breathe and remember that this is one of the ways you are deeply connected to a being that completely *depends* on you and only has this one way of communicating.

That thought can either be helpful or more depressing, but the point is this: crying is not something that is happening *to you* but rather something essential for your child's survival.

Second, the crying can bring to the surface wounds and traumas that we either thought were long gone or never knew existed. I remember a night when my daughter woke up crying several times, and each time it was hysterical. She cried as loudly as she possibly could in all directions, including right into my ear as I held her. Neither I nor her mother knew what to do—a trigger in itself. After weeks of getting little sleep, we were beyond exhausted. We sat in the dark room, deflated, feeling powerless. From what I could tell, my partner seemed to be feeling hopeless. I felt the same, but I also felt a violent anger brewing within. I was angry because *this child wouldn't shut up*. I was angry because I was tired of not getting any sleep. And if I'm being honest, I was also angry at myself for not honoring my partner's initial suggestion to "enjoy your new girlfriend for a bit" when I asked her to give me a child just weeks into our relationship.

I took a deep breath, trying to release the stress from my shoulders and the anger out of my chest. I looked at my daughter and thought about the first time she cried—how sweet that sound was the day she was born. That same cry meant the world to me then. It signaled the end of a long pregnancy, the culmination of months of anticipation, and the beginning of a new and amazing journey. I thought about how innocent that cry was initially and realized how innocent it still was in that harrowing moment. I shifted from being someone upset about having his sleep interrupted to being a dad.

When I finally got a moment of silence to rest, all I could think about was the anger I had felt in that moment. I wondered where that part of me came from—the part that allowed such intense feelings to exist. Right then, I saw my father's face, mixed with anger, looking down at me. I thought of all the times I'd been hit, grabbed, and yelled at. I scanned my memories to find one of being consoled, but I didn't come up with much. I started to hear those stories my dad would share about letting me cry myself to sleep, night after night. I love my dad; I think he's a good man. From the depths of my being, I also know that he had little patience for a crying child, and there were many times when his actions made that very clear.

Most of us don't remember much from our earliest years. The traumas, neglect, and mistreatment that we endured were buried away; they had to be so we could remain connected to the people we relied on to survive. But the memory of these events survives within us, and with the right trigger, we find ourselves face to face with yet another part of ourselves that needs attention and healing. Which takes us back to the feeling of "not knowing what to do."

As a new parent, you may see the following scene many times: you've gone down the list of "to-do's," yet the crying persists. The diaper is dry, the tummy is full, there's no burp to be had, and no *toots* to be freed. You've taken turns rocking the little one until your arms ache, and nothing is doing the trick. You've exhausted all your known options, and now the feeling of being lost is kicking in. You're resting your head on your hand, bewildered and exhausted, and your partner's body language says they are just as spent as you. In that scene, a new parent may feel like they are failing and accept that feeling as truth. But that couldn't be further from reality. The fact that you're giving it your all is what makes you a good parent; not having all the answers doesn't take away from that.

I've been a character in that scene more times than I would like to admit. There was one moment when I felt so dim inside that I looked at my partner and apologized.

"For what?" she asked.

"For placing you in this situation, to begin with."

Before our daughter came into the picture, our life—like yours—was so much simpler. She would take her time preparing delicious dinners, and we would eat in bed while watching our favorite trash TV uninterrupted. We would get high and laugh at jokes we wouldn't remember the next day. And when things got testy or maybe even stale, we could go outside and enjoy a walk that would last as long as we needed. Those are the sweet moments that can leave space for despair when they are no longer within reach. But believe me when I tell you: the moments you weren't sure how you were going to survive—those will also become precious memories someday because you will find that it was those moments that allowed you to see how much of a partner you truly have. Those moments will allow you to grow closer on a much deeper level than you ever could have without them.

And that's what you must remember in those moments—you're in it together. Though it may not be the sort of bliss it was before you saw those two lines on the pregnancy test, you will someday look back on it with the same feelings of nostalgia. If you're reading this with the spit-up of a 3-month-old on your shirt, and you can't fathom this future scenario being likely, I get it. But keep faith that the challenges that seem insurmountable today will become the foundation of a stronger, more resilient relationship—both with your partner and your child.

## *Crying is important.*

One night, not too long ago, I found myself caught in a dream that has lingered with me since. It wasn't intricate or vivid, but it still frightens me the most. In it, my mother was on the phone, her voice trembling as she told me my father had not woken from his sleep. Like most people, the thought of losing a parent stirs a fear unlike any other—a primal dread that reaches deep into the soul. In my dream, I began to weep, and as I did, I felt real tears streaming down the sides of my face. The weight of losing my father, paired with the physical sensation of those tears, began to wake me, pulling me into a hypnagogic state—a space where dream and reality blurred into one.

Still tethered to my dream, I found myself standing in front of my parents. Tears threatened to spill over, but instead of seeking comfort, I turned and walked away, ashamed of my vulnerability. As I regained consciousness, I studied what I had seen and felt in that dreamlike state. Why, at a moment when I should be able to embrace my parents, did I feel compelled to turn away? Why was shame so overpowering? Then, like a sharp gust of wind, the realization started to hit me.

I began seeing myself through my daughter's crying eyes.

I saw flashes of my own anger—how I'd been frustrated, condescending, and dismissive of her tears. And I thought to myself, *who wouldn't feel ashamed to cry in front of someone who reacts that way?* In that instant, I understood that I was not just reacting to my child's emotions—I was replaying my own emotional history. I was a product of what had happened to me. Memories began to resurface, bringing with them the answers I didn't know I had been searching for.

I stared at the ceiling, trying to remember the last time I had cried in front of my parents. Only one moment came to mind: I was a child, sprawled on the side of the road after falling off the bike my father was teaching me to ride. I remembered his face, etched with anger, staring directly into my crying eyes. I didn't see concern or compassion—I saw frustration, maybe even disappointment. And in that moment, all I felt was shame. From that day forward, aside from the occasional whipping, I never cried in front of him again.

For years, I've wondered why crying has always been so difficult for me and why I struggle to allow myself that release. Now, I see it clearly. My ability to cry was blocked, walled off by the emotional inheritance I received from my parents. And now, I see the risk of passing those same blockages to my child.

Crying is vital. Its presence in our evolution proves its importance—it's how we release the weight of emotions that our hearts and minds can no longer bear. It's a physical act of healing, a way to let go. We need to cry, and perhaps more than anything, we need to feel safe crying in front of those we love, especially our parents.

So, Dad, I ask you to join me in something I am challenging myself to do: to run toward the tears, to embrace the flow of emotion, not suppress it, to be the comfort we wish we'd had, not the wall we were made to face. It's time to allow the tears—

for ourselves, for our children, and for the generations that follow.

Whether the issue is great or small, they are crying because they need you.

## *Tips for Surviving the Crying*

1. Go down the checklist. The five basics are hunger/overfeeding, fatigue, discomfort (Such as a dirty diaper or gas), temperature, and pain. Tools like the NoseFrida and Windi are must-haves. They may seem gross to use, but they bring relief to everyone involved and will make for great stories later.

2. Take your time and listen to the cry. We often think babies are poor communicators, but that's not true. Babies and toddlers have their own language, and it's our job to learn it. Most cries are unique; if you take the time to feel the cry, the answer often comes to you. Instead of thinking of how to end the crying, use those cries as a channel to connect with your child and feel what they are feeling in the moment.

3. Don't be afraid to take a break. Despite those judging whispers your mind may generate, taking a moment away from the crying does not make you a bad parent. If you've gone through the checklist and are confident your child can survive a few minutes without your attention, take those minutes. A brief moment of peace can give you what you need to give your child what they need.

4. Remember the first day and the way you felt the first time you heard your child cry. It's the same cry; the only real difference is how you choose to hear it. The first time you heard it, it was something magical, and you can choose to think of it that way again. Sometimes when my daughter cries full-throated in my face, I just look at her and smile. I don't allow the noise to penetrate the part of me that feels anxious, frustrated, or angry. I just look at her and see a little piece of me that has a need, and I go on to do my best to fulfill that need.

# CHAPTER 6

# The Little Things

About twenty percent of couples call it quits by the time their child completes their first trip around the sun. More than half of those still hanging on will experience a significant drop in relationship satisfaction. So, if you're feeling like your life sucks right now, my friend, know this: you are not alone.

It's not hard to find a handful of reasons why parenting can feel like a slog—especially when you're picking from a seemingly endless basket of dirty diapers, unreasonable tantrums, insufferable crying, and guaranteed nights of interrupted sleep. These are the obvious struggles, the ones couples might discuss before embarking on this journey—the ones you can kind of prepare for. What often gets overlooked, though, are the little things that serve as the glue holding you and your partner together, the small rituals that keep you feeling close and connected.

For me, one of those little things was our spontaneous night walks. Before Dahlia came along, my partner and I would take our time circling the block in the evenings, and those moments are something I still find myself missing dearly. Those walks meant so much to our relationship. In fact, it was on our very first walk together that we truly saw each other—saw beyond our representative selves and the small talk. We realized that we were more than just two people who happened to find each other; we were soulmates. Of course, it's worth mentioning we were peaking on LSD at the time—a story I discussed a bit in the first *What She Taught Me*. That walk was born out of a need to break from the weighty discussions about whether to dive into a more intimate relationship. That break was a breath of fresh air. It allowed us to set aside the heaviness of contemplating the future and enjoy a stroll filled with laughter and play.

When the children come, you start to realize just how big those little things were and how vital they are to your relationship. The moment I saw the positive reading on the pregnancy test, was one of the happiest moments of my life. But as the reality sank in, I looked at my partner and asked, "Wait, how long will it be after the baby comes before we can go to the movies again?" The answer, as it turned out, was about two years. What was once a simple, spur-of-the-moment activity to cure boredom became a distant memory, a luxury out of reach.

One by one, the little things I cherished began slipping away. There were the midnight excursions to the beach, the weekends filled with laughter and tears while tripping on mushrooms, the lazy afternoons spent drawing and eating snacks, the uninterrupted trash TV during dinner, and those evening walks to clear our minds. Suddenly, someone had to watch the baby, and those moments became much more difficult to come by— and when we needed them most. Overnight, we were forced to become responsible adults of a new order—a reality we never quite anticipated.

Even having a simple conversation became more of a chore, not just because we were constantly interrupted by Dahlia's needs, including her apparent need to exercise her lungs by crying, but also because we were trying to communicate with much less emotional and mental energy. We started to notice how we spoke to each other had changed. Where did the patience go? What about the softness, the understanding, the kindness—the hanging on to every word to fully receive the message being relayed? What happened to the desire to want to talk through issues rather than brush them aside? All that energy and focus, it turned out, was being redirected to our home's newest addition. When it was just the two of us, we knew what we had to offer each other, and it was amazing. We felt good about what we could offer a child, too. But when you try to give everything to both, you realize just how much trouble you're in.

Without the energy for each other and without the little things that keep you connected, it's easy to find yourself drifting apart. One day, you look up and see a mile of distance between you and the person you once couldn't squeeze a penny between. From there, it's a downhill slide—from staying together just to raise a child to becoming mere roommates to potentially single and co-parenting. This doomsday scenario, however, is avoidable. It requires an intentional focus on nurturing the connection between you and your partner, feeding it whatever it needs to remain strong.

I get it—this isn't easy for everyone, and you never know what life will throw at you during one of your relationship's most stressful and vulnerable periods. Before Dahlia was born, we had grand plans: we would use KidZone at the gym to take breaks, leave her with friends and family while we ran off to play, enroll her in local activities for little ones, and maybe even put her in daycare so we could get back to work and enjoy some midday laziness. But just two months after she was born, a news segment caught my eye—a map of the United States covered in red dots marking new cases of the coronavirus. And just like that, everything changed.

A reality that many new parents face is that you don't know who you are as a parent until you actually become one. Sure, hints of that part of yourself emerge in discussions about a future with children, but it's not until you're living it that you see the full picture. And when you do, you realize the world changes along with you.

By February 2020, the world seemed far less safe than it had before. It wasn't just the pandemic that made me feel this way; it was what I saw of humanity in one of its darker moments. People's personal beliefs and freedoms became more important to them than their own safety and that of others. The world went from a vast place of limitless opportunities to a small, confining space no larger than my yard. Protecting my newborn from this new, more dangerous world became my primary objective. What I learned about myself as a parent was that I was all in, willing to abandon much of what I loved about life—the people and experiences that shaped me up to the day my partner and I met—to keep my child safe. Needless to say, we didn't have much room for the little things, and we paid dearly for it.

The COVID pandemic was my brick wall and my mirror. It took time to shake off the daze, unravel the pressures and expectations I had placed on myself, reorganize my life to benefit my family, and return to the little things that could keep us together. Maybe your child is enough to keep you grounded, but perhaps you've faced your own set of experiences that forced you to rediscover yourself, relearn who you are, and reconnect with your partner.

Parenthood introduces new dimensions of yourself, each with its own wants, needs, and desires—especially concerning your child. Allowing these new parts of yourself to dictate your actions can be costly. The price may be the time, energy, and mental space you'd otherwise dedicate to the little things your relationship once thrived on.

As I reflect on examples from my own life, one that always makes me want to slap my forehead is the decision to buy a house—possibly my biggest misstep since Dahlia was born. My partner and I always speak fondly of the small townhome we used to own—how simple it was, how little we had, and how easy it was to maintain, including the bills. We thought we needed more space once we knew we had a baby on the way. I was eager to leave that townhome and move into a beautiful new home we discovered. It felt like destiny. And it was—if the point was to teach us a hard lesson. I went from having ample time and energy to being stuck mowing the lawn every few days and making frequent trips to the local hardware store to keep the house from falling apart. Not only was I a butler to a newborn, but I had also become a slave to a building. Ironically, I had paused my career to spend more time with my family, but maintaining an old house left me more exhausted than a nine-to-five job. I gave myself permission to provide something I thought my child needed—a big house and a yard to play in—but it cost my family what it needed most: me.

Between trying to keep a house from falling apart and attempting to get my kid to sleep through the night, changing spit-up-stained clothes hourly, and surviving a pandemic, I had little energy left for myself, let alone my relationship. My partner, struggling to hold on herself, was looking for the man she fell in love with—the man I could hardly find myself. This is common among new parents and a major reason many don't make it through those first years together.

But growing apart doesn't have to lead to a breakup, especially when that breakup would have devastating consequences. Growing apart is almost inevitable at times, especially when faced with forces as unforgiving as time and…children. I see an opportunity in the space that has been created between partners: the chance to experience the joy of reunion once more. This is where the work of relationships must begin if you want to finish this journey together. If you're up for it, here are a few thoughts to consider that may help.

First, recognize that while much will change with a child, not everything has to. A new part of yourself opens up during this phase, and that part of yourself has desires tied to your story. What you want to give your child is directly connected to what you had and loved as a child or what you lacked and desperately wanted. Similarly, what you try to prevent your child from experiencing is also tied to your story and may cost you just as much to avoid. You and your partner should carefully consider these new desires and question them before permitting yourselves to pursue them. The temptation to say "yes" will be strong, and the dopamine rush rewarding, but consider the overall cost of such permissions with honesty. One "yes" could place undue stress on the relationship. We didn't question what it would mean to buy an aging house; in fact, I did my best to block out any concerns. We didn't have to sell our simple, cozy little home and move away eight months into a pregnancy. We could have said no to this newfound desire bubbling up from an unfamiliar part of ourselves and kept things simple during those first crucial years of child-rearing. But alas, a few kids raised in trailers grew up wanting more for their child—a nice, big house with a yard that she may or may not care about when she grows up.

Secondly, remember that it's not necessarily the child that causes strain on the relationship—it's the way you and your partner respond. My child is like the Tasmanian Devil, but she's also perfect. She's supposed to cry, throw tantrums, test boundaries, soil her diaper minutes after I've changed it, fight sleep, and toss food on the floor—all things that frustrate me terribly. And don't get me started on the whining. So, it's not reasonable to blame them for the crumbling of relationships, not when we can choose how we relate to our children. By this, I mean we can choose to engage with them in ways that bring everyone less stress, take the time to refill our own cups, and do everything in our power to get back to the little things that keep us connected.

# CHAPTER 7
# Triggers

*"Triggers are teachers. They reveal where we are not free and guide us toward the work we need to do to become liberated."*

— **Jeff Foster**

I had been away from home for a few hours, most likely at the gym, which had become my refuge—my escape from the relentless demands of parenting and the pressures I placed on myself. This evening I came home to a scene that should have felt like a dream come true. The house was bright and clean, Dahlia was watching cartoons, and my partner was in good spirits, humming softly while washing dishes. It was the picture-perfect family moment I'd always envisioned on a good day. I should have been happy, but one part of this picture was off and so unsettling that a quiet anger began to brew within. I tried to keep it at bay, but my energy had already shifted, and a dark cloud began forming over our home.

My partner immediately sensed something was wrong and asked, "What's bothering you?" Of course, my knee-jerk response was, "Nothing is wrong," a phrase that only thickened the tension in the air as the dark cloud took full form. She pressed further, "Tell me what's wrong; what is the matter?" Understandably, she wanted to protect this rare, peaceful scene—a gem that's hard to come by with a toddler around.

But it was already too late. Though I hadn't said what was on my mind, my unsettled state had cast a shadow over the moment. Then it hit her, and I knew it had. I let it out: "Why is Dahlia eating cereal for dinner?"

Her shoulders dropped as she replied, "She's not; it's just a snack." I glanced at the clock, my frustration growing. "A snack before dinner? How much sugar is in that?" The exchange didn't last long but was long enough to ruin the moment. My partner was left feeling like a failure; I was seething with frustration, and Dahlia, confused and upset, sensed the tension. Congratulations, Jereme, you just wrecked a good thing over… cereal.

But, of course, it wasn't really about the cereal. It was a trigger, setting off deeper wounds and fears buried within me.

You never quite know what scene you will walk into when you come home or which part of yourself it will expose. At that moment, I realized that when it came to what Dahlia was eating, I had a big problem—a problem tied to a deep-seated resentment I held toward my own parents for not being more mindful of what I ate as a child. My childhood diet would disgust me today. My dad often laughs about how he used to give me milk bottles to keep me quiet as a baby, and the thought makes me cringe. Night after night, dinner was something fried, something starchy, and if we were good, something sweet. In the mornings, I'd wake up to a bowl of sugary cereal or a stack of pancakes my mom made before rushing to work. I look back on those memories with disgust and nostalgia, but I have yet to let my daughter touch a pancake. Throughout the day, I ate candy with no end. I'd buy hundreds of 1-cent candies from the corner store and make sandwiches out of the hard and soft pieces. When I needed something "real," I'd run home for peanut butter and jelly sandwiches, *heavy on the jelly*. By nineteen, poor eating habits and hygiene had already led me to start losing teeth. By the time I left the military, I was bursting out of my uniform and had no idea why. And at thirty-one, I was diagnosed with pre-diabetes.

For years, I spent thousands trying to keep my smile intact, and at such a young age, I was being told I was at risk for a disease that could have dire consequences if not managed properly. I wasn't just shocked—I was pissed. I took action to undo the damage and start a healthier lifestyle, but along the way, I developed this deep resentment toward my parents. Why didn't they monitor my sugar intake more carefully? Why didn't they ensure my meals were nutritious? Why didn't they teach me the importance of flossing and dental care or prepare me for the health struggles I began to see them face? This resentment was largely inconsequential before I knew I had a baby on the way. It motivated me to make positive changes for myself. However, once I knew she was coming, that resentment turned into an obsession over what my partner was eating while she was pregnant and a gnawing anxiety about not having more control over it. In fact, one reason I couldn't wait for Dahlia to be born was so I could ensure she was getting enough food—and that it was nutritious. I couldn't wait until I could have some level of control.

When she was born, I quickly realized how impossible control is. For example, people love to give children sweets; some do it to warm the child up to them, some do it to see the child smile, and some do both. I also noticed that most, if not all, of these people were suffering from diet-related illnesses themselves, whether they were aware of it or not. Once, we left her with a family member for a few days. When I came home, I made it a point to be the first to check her diaper—just to make sure things were "normal." They weren't. I don't know what she had been fed, but it wasn't anything I would have approved of. At that point, I felt I couldn't trust anyone to follow my specific feeding instructions, so we would just have to keep her to ourselves. And just like that, any chance of a break from parenting to focus on ourselves was mostly axed by my own controlling issues.

As eye-opening as that scene was, I don't think it really hit me until I snatched that Oreo cookie away from her mouth. I shared a little about this before, but it's worth expanding on. Without thinking, I snatched it away before her molars could do their work. As a recovering Oreo addict myself, I know the feeling of anticipating that first bite—the dopamine firing on all cylinders. So, I also knew that Dahlia was heartbroken to see that little black cookie from heaven in my hand instead of her mouth. I stepped outside myself for a moment and watched the whole scene play out, and I had to admit: this is a problem. Sure, I was keeping a lot of sugar from touching my child's tongue, and that's a good thing. But I had to ask myself, is it worth the cost of going this far? Of needing to have this much control? My partner was left feeling like a failure as a parent for not meeting my impossible expectations; her family members were walking on eggshells because they knew "dad is watching," and as a couple, we weren't giving ourselves the time we needed together because I felt the need to monitor my child's eating all day, every day.

It's not worth it.

The scenes that play out in your home will expose you to your triggers, especially when a child is involved. Triggers are not to be feared or shamed; they are simply guides to the parts of yourself that are crying out for attention. They reveal areas of yourself that have been fractured in some way and are in need of repair. I had no idea I had such a strained relationship with food, nor could I fathom that I could be so controlling. But by paying attention to my triggers, I uncovered these truths about myself.

You must allow your triggers to do the same for you. If you want to maintain a healthy relationship with your partner, ensure your children want to visit you when they grow up, keep strong connections with those around you, and, most importantly, move closer to becoming the best possible version of yourself, you must give attention to what your triggers are showing you. This is one of the hidden gifts that comes with the weight of having a family—you now have reliable mirrors reflecting parts of yourself back to you, giving you the opportunity to do something about them. And it's not enough to simply decide to stop the damaging behaviors. I can commit to no longer snatching Oreos out of my daughter's mouth, but the underlying problem will manifest in other ways. When these triggers reveal themselves, you must be willing to go on the journey to their source and healing.

My journey led me to forgive my parents, which became easier once I accepted that they didn't know any better. For instance, my father considers it reasonable to expect dentures by fifty because that was the case for his parents. My mother, bless her stressed soul, has relied on family-sized jugs of soda to get through the day since I was a kid. Besides, they didn't have access to the health information we do today. Once I accepted that, I was able to let go of my resentment. I also realized that I have the resources to be what they couldn't be and the power to do better, which gave me the power to let go of my fear of ending, matching their fate.

Being in control isn't about forcing your environment to bend to your will—that requires a lot of energy and often backfires. In fact, trying to control your environment is a sign that you've lost control. True control is about allowing your environment to be as it is while self-governing in a way that reflects your highest self. Whatever happens outside of you doesn't have to trigger or control you. You have the power to heal so that your triggers become nothing more than passing occurrences. If a trigger points you to a part of yourself that needs healing, you can embark on that journey. If it points you to a part that needs growth, you can go on that journey, too. You also have the option of doing nothing and allowing what ails you to continue thriving within.

You may wonder why someone would hold on to something that keeps them triggered. The irony is, we all do it. As much as some of us like to think we are out of "cares to give," we all tend to keep a number of them on reserve.

There's nothing inherently wrong with that; the problem arises when those cares threaten to blow up your family or perpetuate a cycle of pain that could carry over into your children and grandchildren. We hold onto these parts of ourselves because they have value to us—whether it's the desire to be right, to play the victim, to assert a value, or, in my case, to protect my child's health. In these moments, you must ask yourself, what is more valuable to me? One choice will move you closer to your partner and children, while the other may create more distance.

When it comes to these scenes that expose us to ourselves, it's important to remember that we are always experiencing them through the lenses of our individual stories, composed of the fragments of others' stories we have experienced. When I experience a trigger, I think about the part of my story that has been activated in that moment, and I keep in mind that my response will become a part of someone else's story. There is a narration in your life; you can watch it all play out or take control and dictate the next lines.

And another scene is always on the way.

Recently, I told my partner, "It's not that I don't enjoy being a parent; I just don't enjoy being a parent all the time." It's true, and if you're a parent reading this, you know it's for good reason. One reason is the non-stop of it all; another is the constant stream of unending and unexpected scenes. When you're alone, you have more control over when and how you are confronted with yourself; you have more time to address the issues, and if you don't, the consequences are often far less severe. Those luxuries disappear when you're in a relationship and/or have a child. We see ourselves through our relationships, and once we commit to these kinds of relationships, we can always expect a new scene on the horizon. This is also true because your depth has no bottom. No matter how many doors you open within, there will always be an eternal hallway of them, waiting for an external experience to unlock the next.

# CHAPTER 8

# Protecting the Feminine Energy

*"When a man truly understands the value of the feminine, he will protect it fiercely and nurture it with love."*

– **Unknown**

For yourself, for your children, for your home, and for your relationship—protect feminine energy.

When my partner first stepped into my small townhome, I experienced a revelation about the nature of energy—specifically, the transformative power of feminine energy. The moment she walked in, a magical wave seemed to flood the space, breathing life into every corner of every room. Before that moment, I hadn't realized how stark, colorless, and empty the place had felt. I poured a lot of effort into making the space welcoming for her arrival. I wanted it to be a space where she could see herself living. I spent late nights repainting the walls, rearranging furniture, and tinkering with things I barely understood. If I could make it impressive enough, she'd consider a life with me there.

Yet, despite all my labor, it wasn't the freshly painted walls or the carefully chosen decor that transformed the space—it was her presence. Her energy alone brought warmth and vibrancy to the room, and it struck me how little my efforts had contributed to that feeling. It was as if she filled the house with a kind of magic I could never achieve on my own. When I dropped her off at the airport after her visit and returned to my place, I felt a hollowness that hadn't been there before—or perhaps had always been- but was now glaringly apparent in her absence. Despite all the physical improvements I'd made to the house, it felt like she had taken "home" with her.

That experience opened my eyes to the irreplaceable value of feminine energy. At the time, I wasn't fully aware of what this energy was, but there was a deep knowing within me that it was unique and sacred. It was only over time that I began to understand it more clearly. This energy is the same force that makes flowers bloom in awe, compels lovers to dance under stormy skies, and fearlessly fills spaces where love does not yet exist. It is divine feminine energy—a life-giving force that enriches everything it touches.

## *The Imprint of Presence*

When she left, what remained of her presence was a simple cotton throw she had placed on the sofa. It was my throw, but the way she folded it was hers—a small but significant imprint of her energy. That subtle trace of her spirit was all I had in her absence, and I left it there, untouched, for weeks until she could return with the energy I had come to miss so much. That throw became a small altar, a reminder of the magic she brought into my life and how much her energy had already begun to shape my space.

This experience taught me that nothing is more valuable than feminine energy in a home. It is the well of tenderness, care, and compassion from which your children drink; the sea in which the masculine finds peace and renewal; the rain of flavor breathes life into everything it touches, transforming a mere house into a home. Without it, everything begins to fall apart—a truth that we too often forget in our busy lives.

## *Balancing Feminine and Masculine Energies*

When my partner moved in, we discussed how we would handle finances and responsibilities. She was free to work, but I wanted her to have the freedom to pour her energy into the home if she chose. Having lived a life of independence up to that point, it wasn't surprising that she chose to work anyway. There's nothing inherently wrong with that decision; many women find fulfillment in their careers. However, over time, many begin to experience what so many families around the world face: the gradual decline of feminine energy in the home.

The rise of capitalism has created a reality where both masculine and feminine energies are often left at the office, traded for a paycheck. The home, meant to be a sanctuary, becomes another place where people sleep and store their things. A lack of either energy leaves the home vulnerable to various challenges that creep in unnoticed. When feminine energy is depleted or diverted elsewhere, the consequences can ripple throughout the household. A man may seek from other women what is missing in his house; children may feel emotionally disconnected and seek validation elsewhere. A house devoid of feminine energy reflects this absence both energetically and visibly. It lacks connection, compassion, and warmth, and therefore, it lacks the foundation needed to stand strong for long.

This is why feminine energy in the home should be protected at all costs—there is no price higher than the value of the feminine.

## *The Modern Challenge*

When my partner began working, there was an initial excitement—the kind that often comes with a new job, new colleagues, and a new environment. But as time went on, the demands of work increased, and so did the drain on her energy—energy that could have gone toward nurturing our relationship, fostering a warm atmosphere, and deepening our connection. This is what most jobs do to us: they strip away not just our time but our creative and connecting energy, leaving us with little left for our partners or our homes. This is especially true for the feminine when the workplace is heavily masculine—that is, task-oriented, highly structured, and often mindlessly repetitive.

While the feminine can operate within a masculine structure, it can also be draining—especially when that relationship with the masculine does not involve intimacy, creativity, or a deeper sense of purpose. Imagine being a free-flowing river of energy forced to operate within the rigid boxes of time, documentation, offices, procedures, dress codes, and the mask of professionalism all day. It's a lot to ask of someone who is dominantly feminine. It's not just about doing the work; it's also about the suppression of a core part of oneself that makes life more exhausting than it needs to be. This isn't to say women can't thrive in male-dominated fields—they absolutely can and do. But it does mean we need to be mindful of how much of ourselves we give away to structures that don't nourish us.

I watched this dynamic play out in my own home growing up. One of my father's fatal flaws was allowing my mother to take on the primary financial responsibility while he contributed as he pleased. For reasons unknown to me, he chose to retire during his prime working years, leaving my mother to bring in consistent paychecks while he dabbled in his talents, curiosities, and hobbies. One of my earliest memories is the sound of my mother's high heels clicking against the hall floors as she prepared to leave for work around 5:30 a.m. That was my cue that I had about an hour before I needed to get up for school. By the time she returned, the sun would already be flirting with the horizon.

For years, my mother maintained this grueling routine. When I was a child, her energy felt sweet and nurturing, but as the years went on and she shouldered more of the financial burden, that sweetness began to fade. What replaced it was a bitterness born from years of working in a masculine-dominated career that drained her. By the time she retired, she was just that—tired, exhausted in a way that permeated every part of her being.

As a child, I couldn't fully understand the reason for the change, but it became painfully clear that much of the energy we all missed had been left in a seat she occupied for 8 to 10 hours a day for a company that gave her as little as they could get away with in return. A job that required her to trade her vital energy for a paycheck that barely covered our needs. It wasn't just the job that took a toll on her; it was also the emotional toll of feeling undervalued, both in the workplace and, perhaps, at home.

## *A Wise Approach to Protecting Feminine Energy*

A wise partner, regardless of gender, understands the value of the energy their counterpart brings to the home and does what is necessary to protect it. This may involve her working a job that pays less but allows her to thrive in her feminine energy throughout the day or pursuing her own interests that recharge her spirit while she works. There are many solutions, but in a society where consumption seems to be the ultimate goal, pursuing material things can often get in the way of protecting your home's most valuable resource: the divine feminine energy.

Another mistake my father made was leaving most of the homemaking duties to my mother. Homemaking is about more than keeping a space clean; it's about designing and maintaining the sanctuary that the family occupies. When all this work falls on one person—especially after a long day of employment—it drains the very energy everyone benefits from. I remember my mother coming home from long hours at work, only to immediately start her second shift: cleaning the house and preparing dinner. Everything suffers when energy is drained. I never knew my mother to be much of a cook, but I came to realize it wasn't because she lacked skills; it was because she didn't have much left in the tank.

When it comes to homemaking, many men are resistant to taking on a more active role. Perhaps this is because, deep down, we recognize how menial, time-consuming, and energy-draining these tasks can be. Instead of resisting, we should use that understanding to empathize and take a more significant role in sharing these responsibilities. This way, her energy can be used to enhance her relationship with herself, her relationship with us, and the overall health of the home.

By now, you might be asking yourself, "Must I do everything?" And the truth is, depending on the type of lifestyle you desire, much may be required to keep both masculine and feminine energies balanced and thriving in your home. For the masculine, losing sight of the dance can be easy because we're so caught up in making sure the dance floor is sturdy. In other words, we place a great deal of our energy on the structure—the home, the finances, the external threats that could impact the home. While this is necessary, we can find ourselves so engulfed in protecting and maintaining the floor that we lose connection to the feminine, and eventually, we lose the dance as well. We must do both. It is how we suffer for what we love.

*The Dance*

This chapter may seem like a bit of a departure from the rest of the book, but it is more in line with *What She Taught Me*, where I thoroughly discussed the value of both masculine and feminine energies. The subject is worth revisiting because of how easily we tend to lose sight of the importance of the energy our partner brings. If we take it for granted, we needlessly lose so much of it. We collect responsibilities along the journey of a relationship, and many of those responsibilities chip away at the energy in the home—especially the responsibilities that come with raising children.

You want your children to have their mother's sweet energy; you want to walk into that energy every day when you come home. You need to be filled with it through connection. The well has a limited supply, so one of the most important things you and your partner can do together is ensure that the well does not run dry.

For families to thrive, there must be a conscious effort to create a balance that respects both partners' energies. This involves communication, empathy, and a willingness to rethink traditional roles. It's not about returning to some outdated model but about evolving into a partnership where both people feel valued, seen, and supported.

If we, as partners, can protect and nurture the feminine energy in our homes—whether by creating an environment where she feels valued or by sharing responsibilities more equitably—we not only enrich our relationships but also create a more nurturing and loving space for our children. In doing so, we build homes that are not just shelters but sanctuaries—places where both partners can thrive and grow together.

# CHAPTER 9

# Closer, or Further?

*"A person's a person, no matter how small."*

**– Dr. Seuss**

My interactions with my parents are occasional. I visit them maybe five or six times a year and try to make it a point to call at least once a week to check in. But when we talk, it often feels like a ritual more than a meaningful exchange. The conversations are mostly one-sided. Either I'm serving as a cushioned toilet seat for my mom to unload all that's been piling up in her life, or I'm nodding along as my dad discusses his latest ventures in real estate, or something involving religion. I've learned to keep what I share with them to just the basics. Over time I've grown to realize that they never seemed particularly interested in my journey. Maybe I'm wrong, but that's how it has felt. And so, I've made peace with it.

With time, I've noticed that my perception of them has changed. They're less "Mom and Dad" to me now and more like people I have a history with—people I care about deeply but don't necessarily feel understood by. It fascinates me how, at one point in our lives, our parents are our entire world, and then, as time passes, so much space develops between us that it feels like a vast ocean. We drift, but we don't always know why.

When I think about what caused that distance for me, one memory surfaces immediately: the scene of my father hitting me on the back of the neck with a cable cord. The cord was a departure from the usual switch or belt he'd use, and perhaps that's why it stands out so vividly in my mind.

By then, my father and I had been at odds for some time. I don't recall the exact reasons, but I can guess—I was likely going through a phase as a teenager that triggered something in him, and he was grappling with his own challenges as a father that, in turn, triggered me. Tension was building like a pressure cooker, and one night, it all came to a head.

I had taken a cable cord from behind his TV to use for mine. When he came looking for it, I gave it back reluctantly and with an attitude—two things my dad never took well. Something snapped in him. My father had whipped and spanked me for as far back as I can remember, sometimes leaving welts all on my body. I thought I knew what was coming, but I was wrong.

He swung the cable cord and struck me on the back of my neck. It felt like I had been sliced open to the bone; I'd never felt anything more painful. He then rushed me onto my bed and unleashed a series of punches to my body. I could tell he wasn't punching with his full strength, but just the fact that my father—my protector—was hitting me like that caused something deep inside me to shatter. I tried to guard myself as best I could. At that age and size, I could have fought back, but I knew I could never bring myself to hit my father. Even if I could, it would only make things worse.

I could feel his anger and frustration pouring out with every hit, and I knew that the source of it was much deeper than what was going on between us. I could also sense the regret creeping in as the power behind his punches waned. We've never spoken about it since, but sometimes I wonder if, in that moment, he had a flashback to holding me as a baby, marveling at my tiny hands, and wondering how he could ever harm his own child.

When he finally let me up, I felt an anger inside me so intense that it completely took over. I knew I couldn't hurt him physically, but I was certain I could wound him with my words. I looked into the eyes of the man who adopted me as a baby and took me in as his own—the man who spun me like an airplane and tickled me into breathless laughter as a small child, who I stood next to in church mimicking his every move during songs, who had sacrificed so much to provide for me—and I yelled, "I hate you! I have a gun, and I'm going to blow your fucking head off!"

It's incredibly difficult to place myself back in that moment. Sure, my anger was justified. Maybe my words were a fitting punishment for his actions. But to this day, I feel like I was a terrible son and a terrible human being. The guilt has stayed with me, lingering like a shadow I can't shake.

At that moment, I was sure my father would unleash an even greater fury on me, but he didn't. Instead, being a man of the church, he turned to that version of himself. He wrapped his arms around me in a sudden embrace and said, "This is what the devil doesn't want us to do." That was when I knew he felt guilt and shame, masking it with talk of some evil presence or being. All the pain I had bottled up inside came pouring out through my tears. I realized then that all I really needed was a hug from my dad.

I couldn't remember the last time I'd gotten one. That hug meant the world to me. But at that moment, being so close had become less of a comfort and more of a reminder of how much damage he could inflict. I learned then that in the face of such conflict, we have two choices: to act in a way that brings us closer together or in a way that creates distance. The way my father chose distance that night, I felt I had no choice but to respond in kind. To the core of my being, I could no longer see him as a safe place.

In much of my writing over the years, I found a way to weave in my thoughts on corporal punishment, not only because I am so vehemently against it but because I want parents to understand how it is one of many acts that can create a vast divide between them and their children. As children, we have experiences that cause us to distance ourselves from our parents. We may even swear to never commit the same offenses. And yet, somewhere along the way, we lose that wisdom and find ourselves justifying and repeating those acts. Then, like our parents, we wonder why our children grow up, move away, and keep just enough contact to maintain the semblance of a relationship—or they completely cut the parent off.

When I talk to believers of corporal punishment, I am always met with the same question: "What would you do instead of hitting in this situation?" And, of course, the situation presented is always an extreme outlier. My answer is often, "I don't know." But what I do know is that in such situations, it is always best to come up with a solution that is not only effective but also brings us closer together rather than driving us apart.

Dr. Jordan Peterson once shared a piece of advice that I hold close: "More than anything, our children want to be close to us. Because of that, we have the opportunity to have the best relationship we can possibly have with any human on this planet." After he offered that advice, his face flushed, and tears fell from his eyes. He looked like a man who realized he either succeeded in keeping that closeness or failed to do so and knew exactly why.

Peace can easily exist in a home without children, between people who enjoy spending time together. But a child can be an agent of chaos, capable of causing a scene at any given moment. They will push boundaries, frustrate you, and dance on your last nerve. They want to be close to you but will often give you every reason to do something that drives you further apart. And sometimes, you will. In those moments, I ask myself to do one thing: something I can be proud of. That might mean showing love, compassion, and patience, or it could mean simply walking away because I don't know what to do or because I feel I am losing control. It proves far better than a quick reaction that could create a chasm in our connection.

"Closer or further?" is what I keep in mind when managing conflict—of which there will always be a plentiful supply in a family unit. What I've learned is that simply ruling out a harmful behavior isn't enough to achieve the end result you're looking for. The parent you wish to be and the connection you imagine having with your child requires a journey of investigation, learning, and growth.

Here's the scene that inspired this thought. My daughter and I were at the gym; I was desperately ready to work out, and she was looking at the entry to the "kids zone" with an expression that read, "I'm not going in there." I know my child, and I saw it coming. She had been giving me trouble from the moment we got out of the car to taking a picture for the front desk, so I knew the version of her that says "no" to everything was making an appearance. I was more frustrated than usual because before we left home, I had asked her very clearly whether she wanted to stay home or go play with the other kids at the gym. Not only did she say yes, but she also ran to the door as fast as she could to put her shoes on. When she slipped her heel into the second shoe, she perked up like fresh toast and said, "I'm ready, Daddy." But somewhere along the seven-mile drive to the gym, something changed. *Toddlers.*

I stood there with the door open, gently telling her it was time to walk in. Each time I did, she took a step back. Every step back she took, my frustration and impatience grew. Finally, I knelt down to her level and offered an ultimatum: "Kids zone or time-out—which one?" She chose time-out. Damn. The last thing I wanted was to spend the next five minutes waiting for her to tap out of time-out and go play so I could work out. Eventually, she did just that. I'm sharing this scene to admit that I didn't feel good about it. In fact, for the entire workout, I felt guilty. I didn't know why I felt so bad, but I knew I had done something wrong.

My workout goal for the day was two hours of cardio, legs, and back. I made it about halfway through before I had to pick up my daughter just to say I was sorry. When she saw me enter the kids zone, she did what she always does. She took a few steps back, then sprinted toward me and shouted as loud as she could, "Daaaadddaaaayyyyyy!" It's something that melts my heart every time. When she does it, I hope to the heavens it's not the last time. I opened my arms for her embrace, and for that moment, time stood still. This time, I picked her up and said, "Sweetheart, Daddy is sorry for putting you in time-out. That wasn't fair of me." Sometimes, I'm not sure if she understands me—after all, she was just three years old at the time. But she replied, "And I'm sorry that I was scared to go into the kids zone, Daddy." Right then, I realized what I had done wrong: I didn't listen. And to make matters worse, I abused a tool of correction, forcing her to do what I wanted. That was when I decided that punishment would always be a last resort.

Dr. Gabor Maté, a world-renowned physician and author who specializes in child development, once said something that struck me: "Our children learn that we don't want them around us when they experience intense feelings," and "automatically isolating them deprives them of a chance to practice being active, empathetic decision-makers who are empowered to figure things out." I wasn't actively seeking this advice—I just came across it while scrolling the internet. It wasn't something I wanted to accept, either, as time-outs were something I found useful, and the last thing I wanted was to have that challenged with a good argument. But when this scene presented itself and I failed miserably, those words came back to me, and I began to understand what he meant. In a moment when I could have grown closer to my daughter simply by listening, I chose to act in a way that could have (and may have) caused us to grow apart.

If anyone deserved a time-out, it was me. As parents, we must be honest with ourselves about who is in the wrong in any given conflict. We pay now by facing the truth of ourselves, or we pay later with a distant relationship with the people we brought into the world.

*What do I do?*

Since I started this journey of challenging parents to consider how they relate to their children, many have come to me seeking advice on tough situations, especially when they are trying to avoid corporal punishment. I have a complicated relationship with this question because it's almost impossible to answer. There are so many reasons why a child may behave in a way that is unfavorable to the parent, and so many ways a parent might perceive it or find themselves triggered by it. There are also countless ways a situation can be handled. What I often receive is something akin to, "My child won't stop fighting in school; what should I do? I don't want to hit him, but his dad thinks we should, and I am starting to agree because I don't know what else to do." This is just one of the questions I've received, and it's almost impossible to answer without a great deal of context. What is happening at school? What is happening at home? What is the quality of the parent-child relationship? And so on. The answer I am often forced to give—and I really hate to—is, "I don't know." In fact, many times, I stand in front of my own child telling myself the same thing.

What I advise parents to do is to start by eliminating what they know does not work—at least if the goal is to resolve the conflict without causing harm to the relationship.

What tops my list of what doesn't work is hitting. Empirical research, such as a 50-year study published by The University of Texas at Austin and the University of Michigan, concludes that the risks of corporal punishment far outweigh any perceived rewards. Those risks include psychological and physiological harm, stunted development, anxiety, depression, substance abuse, and antisocial behaviors. To me, that should be more than enough reason to sway any well-meaning parent from resorting to hitting, because I find it hard to believe that any well-meaning parent truly wants to harm their own child.

It's also off the list for me because, as a man, I understand the messages I am sending by using physical violence as a tool to correct a child. Those messages are that violence is an acceptable solution for conflicts that do not involve self-defense and that love can be intertwined with physical violence. Both are unacceptable in my view.

What follows is force. As much as possible, I try to avoid force, because doing so often leads to a power struggle where there is no winner. Even if I manage to bend my child to my will by force, it may come at the cost of our connection. There's also the reality that some things can't be forced. A child cannot be forced to sleep, eat, poop, or stop crying. But they can be given a full day so that they are ready for bed; they can have a feeding regimen and foods they are excited to eat; their feelings can be validated, and they can be listened to. These are all much better options than tactics of force, which often involve some level of violence or abuse.

When you don't know what to do, my advice is to do nothing. What is important to remember, especially in tense situations, is that you don't have to act right away. If you feel that you do, question that.

A classic example is a temper tantrum in a store. Many parents feel the need to resolve the situation immediately with some kind of force, which only makes things worse. It often leads to a shortened trip and a car full of angry people. Many times, the reason the parent feels the tantrum needs to be ended quickly has little to do with the child's behavior and more to do with the embarrassment the parent is feeling in the moment. As with any tantrum, the child is expressing big feelings in a way they haven't yet learned to regulate, and instead of mirroring how to do so, the parent begins to unravel as well. Not doing anything gives you time to think about the next actions, to ensure that they will strengthen connection, trust, and boundaries. It's a golden opportunity to teach when you allow yourself time to be the teacher rather than a bully.

Acknowledge that you don't know. Many parents operate on default mode, continuing the parenting styles of their parents or making guesses as they go. Even worse, many of us can become defensive when our parenting styles are challenged. Much of this job has already been experienced, studied, researched, learned the hard way, solved, and shared with the public. Take advantage of it. However many tools you think you have, there are, in fact, many more. Some of those tools are more aligned with the result you're looking for than the tools you are currently using.

# CHAPTER 10

# They Are What They Are Supposed to Be

Fruit trees don't care about us. You may have never wondered whether they do or not, but considering how much they provide for us, perhaps it's worth pondering. Fruit trees contribute greatly to a healthy ecosystem. They produce fresh oxygen, provide a habitat for wildlife, and yield delicious, nature-made candies we love so much. I can hardly get my daughter to eat anything without mixing in some fruit, and I can always count on her asking, "Can I have a banana?" the moment after she's finished devouring one.

But how could a life form that offers us an endless supply of sweet, succulent treats not care for us? The answer lies in the true purpose of fruit. For the tree, the flesh of the fruit itself is not what's important. The true purpose is the seed within—the tree's means of procreation. The tree doesn't invest so much time and energy into creating the sweet flesh surrounding the seed because it likes us. It does so to entice us, or any creature, to transport and drop the seed far away, giving it a chance to grow without competing with the mother tree for resources.

This natural process can shed light on why your toddler keeps dropping food on the floor despite your many attempts to stop them. Yes, sometimes they do it to test boundaries, protest, or demand attention, but at its core, this behavior stems from generations of natural contributions to our surrounding ecosystem. It's the same reason they pee and poop at will, why they seem to destroy everything they can get their little hands on, and why they feel compelled to climb and jump all over your good furniture—it's all just natural programming.

The complex structures we live within today bear little resemblance to the environments humanity has spent hundreds of thousands of years adapting to. When we strip ourselves down to the basics, we're just like every other animal: born to eat, sleep, seek safety, and procreate. Over time, we've created structures that can be seen as both gifts and curses—language, time, education, the workforce, inventions designed to make life easier, and, to tie this to my point, civility. Just about everything we consider civil is something we made up, and when we become parents, we realize just how much work it is to indoctrinate into the next generation.

Ejecting food that's not liked and lifting a plate only to dump its contents on the floor—these are all natural behaviors. But kindly spitting food into a napkin and disposing of it, placing utensils neatly on a plate while saying, "I'm done"—these are civil behaviors. As parents, we're not just training our little ones to thrive within these societal structures; we're also fighting against an inconceivably long history of nature doing its part. Babies don't come into the world with a blank slate; they arrive running on a program that will take time and effort to reshape. So much of what may be wrecking your nerves is exactly what they're supposed to be doing.

Viewing your role as a parent through this lens can significantly help with patience. It may open you up to a level of understanding that allows you to be a little kinder about the things that typically exhaust and irritate you. Nothing irks me more than catching my child mid-flight from the highchair to the couch. But then I remind myself: she's just doing what little monkeys do. At that point, I don't have to feel as upset about it, and really, that's all I need. Besides, when you give them negative feedback, they learn exactly what to use against you when they *do* purposely want to get on your nerves.

We tend to give more grace to other humans when they're doing what we perceive as normal. If a baby is wailing on a plane, it might disturb you, but you probably have the patience for it because that's what babies do. But if a 40-year-old man made the same sounds, you'd be looking for the flight crew to tape his mouth shut. That might be an exaggeration, but, you get the point. Yet, if you found out that the 40-year-old man had severe Tourette's Syndrome, your patience might return. Our understanding of what's "normal" behavior dictates how we react.

When my daughter turned two, I waited anxiously for the terror I'd heard about to arrive. It came a little late, but when it did, I understood why it was labeled as such. As challenging as it was, I decided to do my best not to view the experience as a terror but rather as an opportunity to help a new-to-the-world, uncivilized little being. As with any event you face, you can change how you experience it by simply changing your thoughts about it. What we call "the terrible twos" is simply an opportunity to mold our children into someone we will like and someone who we feel will be good for themselves and the world. Changing how we think about this experience changes our relationship to it, and a better relationship with a challenging experience creates more opportunities to grow closer where we might have been driven further apart.

*There are more gifts this whirlwind of an experience offers.*

A child is the closest thing to perfect that we know. That's why, no matter where you go, your little one causes people to pause and marvel. By just being children, they bring smiles to stoic faces and soften hardened hearts. Accepting their purity is acknowledging that the conflicts that arise are lights shining on parts of ourselves that need our attention. When I call my daughter and she responds with "What?" my blood boils just a bit. But why? Not only is it an appropriate response, but it's also how I often respond to her when she calls for me. The rise in my temperature is there solely because of my parents and grandparents' emphasis on saying "sir" and "ma'am" when addressing adults. It was so important to them that we could be punished for even mistakenly responding with "What?" Long before my daughter was born, I chose not to pass on the tradition of "ma'am" and "sir" because of its roots during slavery in America, but it wasn't until I was hit with a "What?" that I felt the sting of that commitment. Many such issues will arise during this intense stage of parenting—all opportunities for you to create a better person out of yourself, which will, by default, make you a better partner and parent for your family.

It was a startling realization that I wasn't as patient as I believed myself to be, nor as kind or attentive. I was surprised to discover that I could be so paranoid about being taken advantage of, that I am controlling, and that I had grown so disconnected from my inner child that I struggled to connect with my little one. These were just some of the parts of myself that this experience revealed to me—opportunities to become someone I can be even more proud of.

There are amazing qualities this experience will reveal about yourself, and there will be many areas to work on as well. Many people choose the route of bludgeoning themselves with the self-truths they don't like, which is an option. But you can also choose to see them as opportunities, follow the journey they lead you on, and create a better life in doing so.

Another gift I want to reference is the gift of resilience and the knowledge that you have someone with whom you can face the harsh realities of life. As of this writing, my partner and I have been together for five years, and we have either been pregnant or raising a child for all five of them. There aren't many days that go by when I don't, without an ounce of guilt, think about what our relationship would be like without a child. Of course, I have no way of knowing, but I imagine we would still be where we were—happy together, without too many cares in the world. I know that without the many tests we've faced during this time, our relationship wouldn't have the depth and resilience it has today. Back then, I looked at her adoringly because of her beauty, kindness, and the energy of fresh love. Today, I adore her even more because of what I have seen her endure and how we have survived even the toughest moments together.

The experience of raising a child will offer countless opportunities for distance in all your relationships, but each one also offers a chance to grow closer. To make it a little easier, remember that your child is doing what they're supposed to do, and so are you. Whatever you feel and think as a result of what your little one naturally does, you are supposed to feel and think. Whether it's regret, frustration, excitement, anxiety, or joy, these are all doors leading to a room within you that holds a part of yourself worth exploring.

# CHAPTER 11

# Your Values Are Your Responsibility

*"It is not what you leave to your children, but what you leave in your children."*

— **Shannon L. Alder**

In this scene, I find myself rooted in the center of what was once my living room, now engulfed in a riot of chaos created by my daughter's boundless energy. The space, typically a sanctuary of minimalist calm, has been transformed into a battlefield of childhood exuberance. Every corner is strewn with a colorful array of toys—stuffed animals lie toppled over like tiny casualties, plastic blocks form precarious towers, and dolls lay abandoned, their vacant eyes staring up at the ceiling. Blankets, once neatly folded, are now draped over furniture. Books, many of them her favorites, lay splayed open on the floor, their pages torn away by her relentless curiosity. And then there are the clothes—small, mismatched socks, tiny shirts, and pants, tossed about like confetti, creating a mosaic of her presence across the room.

As I take in the scene, I feel the tension rising within me, a palpable force that tightens my chest and sets my nerves on edge. The minimalist in me, the part that craves order and simplicity, is silently screaming in protest. The once serene space now feels like it's closing in, the clutter encroaching on my sanity, threatening to overwhelm me with its sheer volume. My pulse quickens, each beat a reminder of the chaos that has taken over, and I can feel the anxiety bubbling up, dangerously close to boiling over.

And then I see her—my daughter, the little whirlwind responsible for this symphony of disorder. She stands at the epicenter of it all, a pint-sized tornado, utterly absorbed in her own world. Her small hands clutch a bright red ball, and with a look of fierce determination, she winds up and hurls it into the air. The ball soars high above the mess she's created. As it reaches its peak, she turns to me with a smile so radiant, so full of innocent pride, that it's almost impossible to remain frustrated. Her eyes sparkle with the expectation of praise as if she's just achieved something monumental, something that deserves a standing ovation.

If I were a cartoon character, this would be the moment where my face would turn a vivid shade of candy apple red, steam would shoot out of my ears in exaggerated puffs, and my body would quiver with the effort of containing my frustration. But I'm not a cartoon; I'm a father, standing in his living room, trying to keep it together. So instead of exploding, I take a deep breath, forcing my expression to remain as neutral as possible. Inside, though, my thoughts race, and I repeat to myself like a mantra:

## "Don't mess up a good scene, don't mess up a good scene."

The "good scene" being my daughter's radiant smile, a beacon of innocence and joy. This is what I chose to focus on, but beneath that smile, there was a lot that triggered me—like the scattered toys strewn everywhere. I'll tell you why. Before becoming a parent, I heard countless times that having children changes everything—a truth I was determined to defy. But seeing her scattered toys was like a stark reflection. Accepting this truth meant accepting that the quiet and simple life I enjoyed before parenthood was over.

To add, I had told her many times not to throw things in the house, yet there she was, gleefully tossing a ball high into the air as if I'd never said a word. A surge of frustration rose within me, driven by that part of myself that couldn't stand being disobeyed—a part shaped by my father, who could not tolerate any instance of disobedience. That part of me was ready to explode.

But there she stood, with an incredible smile stretched from ear to ear, beaming with pride at how high she could throw the ball. At that moment, I made a choice: to see her joy and to focus on what mattered most. The last thing I wanted was for her happiness to be crushed by my inability to manage my own triggers—triggers that probably exist because someone else, when handling me as a child, failed to manage theirs.

So, I took a breath and calmly asked her not to throw things in the house. Then, I stepped away, giving myself a moment to let my racing thoughts settle and my anxiety-laden body to relax. I wanted to savor her joy and the beauty of the moment, but first,

I had to confront the challenge it brought me—a chance to examine the part of myself that was standing in the way of truly enjoying my child.

The trigger sent my thoughts spiraling. *"Jereme, why on earth did you decide to have a child? Remember the peace of living alone?"* Frustration boiled over as my mind fixated on the idea of a life apart from my family. The more I entertained that thought, the clearer it became: I needed to change my thinking before I lost myself completely—because deep down, I knew there was a part of me that would never allow me to walk away from them. Entertaining the idea only created friction inside, which made everything worse.

Being part of a family forces you to confront your triggers, many of which you might not even realize exist. My daughter, like most toddlers, is a little whirlwind, leaving a trail of chaos in her wake. Before I know it, there are messes in every corner of the house, and I find myself overwhelmed, my head buried in my hands. In those moments, I want nothing more than to retreat to a clean, quiet corner and hide until I can think and feel my way out. But rather than just letting the thoughts and emotions pass, I chose to dig deeper. Were these feelings even mine, or were they inherited patterns? Were they serving me, or were they on the verge of tearing apart the life I've worked so hard to build? Were they stopping me from being the father and partner I aspired to be?

Triggers are opportunities in disguise—a sore spot lying dormant until an event touches it, directing us to parts of ourselves that demand attention. They often serve as a bridge to our own childhoods, bringing back memories of experiences with our parents that may have created distance, misunderstanding, or even a sense of emotional separation. These reactions are rarely about the present moment; instead, they are echoes of the past, unresolved feelings resurfacing in the moment.

In a family setting, particularly when raising children, triggers become a mirror, reflecting the patterns and behaviors we might unconsciously inherit and project. They serve as vital warnings, reminding us that we may be on the brink of repeating the same cycles—echoes of the parenting styles we were subjected to, the same mistakes our parents may have made, and the same gaps in emotional connection. Left unchecked, these triggers have the potential to create the very distance we fear most, to fracture the bonds with our children in much the same way they fractured our connections with our own parents.

But when we recognize triggers for what they are, they become powerful tools for growth. They challenge us to confront uncomfortable truths about ourselves, understand where these reactions come from, and, crucially, decide whether we want to continue living by them. By seeing them not as threats but as opportunities for healing, we can begin to break free from the cycles that bind us, choosing instead to forge a new path—one that fosters closeness, understanding, and authentic connection with our children.

When triggered into a whirlwind of destructive thoughts, I often found myself pointing fingers, blaming my partner for what had happened or for how I felt at that moment. It was deeply unfair and undeniably destructive. This kind of dynamic can become a toxic undercurrent in co-parenting, easily eroding the foundations of a relationship and slowly tearing a family apart. Blame can feel like a reflex, a way to deflect from the uncomfortable truth: we are responsible for giving ourselves what we desire. Acceptance of this truth brings us closer to actualizing our wants, while blaming others for those desires that do not manifest only deepens the divide in the relationship.

To see this more clearly, let's step back for a moment. About ten minutes before the scene I described, I was waking up from a midday nap. Imagine that disorienting shift from rest to chaos—a messy room, a toddler in perpetual motion—it felt overwhelming, to say the least. Just a month earlier, I shared my need for a tidy, calm environment with my partner, and we agreed to help our daughter learn to clean up before moving from one play area to the next. Yet, at this moment, all those good intentions collided with the reality of a triggering scene, and I stood at a crossroads: I could lose my temper completely or lean into the discomfort, looking inward to create an environment where everyone, eventually, gets what they need.

And this is where the real lesson lies: your values are your responsibility, as are the triggers that accompany them. How you choose to manage these triggers will not only shape your own reality but also profoundly influence the lives of your family. The way you respond to these internal challenges—whether with patience and introspection or with frustration and blame—sets the tone for your household, guiding the emotional landscape in which your family lives. By owning your values and the triggers they bring, you take control of the ripple effect they create, fostering an environment where growth, understanding, and connection can flourish.

In these moments, it's tempting to lash out and demand that others—especially our partners—understand and prioritize our needs. But expecting our partners to be as focused on what we want for our child as we are can be unrealistic. It's unfair, and it can create a sense of distance in a relationship where love and cooperation should be the foundation.

Each of us carries a unique blend of experiences, values, and triggers into our relationships—a collection of beliefs and emotional responses shaped by our individual paths. These elements form the fabric of who we are, stitched together by the lessons we've learned, the pain we've felt, and the joys we've experienced. They are like the fingerprints of our emotional lives—no two are exactly the same, and each tells a story that is ours alone.

Yet, in the intimacy of a partnership, we often find ourselves wanting our partner to see things exactly as we do, to share the same urgency and passion for what we deem important. This desire, while understandable, overlooks a fundamental reality of our partner's individuality. They, too, have their own needs and battles to fight, their own stories that shape their reactions and beliefs. Expecting them to feel as strongly about our values as we do is not just unrealistic—it's unfair. It's asking them to abandon their own emotional landscape to inhabit ours, to carry the weight of our triggers alongside their own.

Our triggers are deeply personal. They are ours to own, to explore, and to manage. They often spring from unresolved parts of our past—those invisible threads woven through our lives, waiting to be pulled. When we make the mistake of insisting that our partner should naturally share our emotional responses, we not only set them up to fail, but we also risk building resentment and distance in the relationship. It's not that they don't care; it's that they haven't walked our exact path and haven't felt the precise emotions tied to our experiences.

By recognizing that our triggers belong to us, we allow our partners the freedom to be themselves, to parent and to navigate family life in their own way. This doesn't mean they won't support us, but it acknowledges that they may support us differently from their own authentic place. It gives them room to contribute to our shared goal of raising a healthy, happy child without the constant pressure of meeting expectations that don't originate from within them.

When we understand and respect this, we create a more compassionate and flexible family dynamic. We honor the differences in our values and triggers, allowing room for both of us to grow individually while still nurturing the bonds that keep us together as a family. This approach fosters resilience in our relationship—it becomes less about demanding alignment in every instance and more about finding balance, understanding, and mutual respect. It's about accepting that we are two different people with two different stories, choosing to build a life together despite those differences, and often, because of them.

Seeing our child's toys scattered across the floor feels like I'm being buried under a mountain of 'stuff,' each piece weighing on me with invisible force. My chest tightens, and my thoughts spiral—visions of an endless future flash before me, where I'm forever cleaning up after another person, my days filled with a ceaseless cycle of picking up, sorting, and tidying. It's a fear deeply rooted, passed down like a family heirloom, from my mother's anxieties about keeping a spotless house. Her life has been a relentless battle against chaos, even as we grew into adults.

I remember the regret in her eyes, the sorrow etched in the lines of her face as she lay in that hospital bed, nearing 70, reflecting on a life that did not include much living for herself. Her story became a part of mine.

I know my partner supports the idea of keeping our daughter's things in place, but I also understand that this need, this visceral reaction, is deeply personal. For her, the scattered toys are simply a temporary mess, a natural consequence of a child at play. For me, they are echoes of the past, a reminder of the battles my mother fought and a life I fear. Unless she feels this on the level I do, it will never carry the same weight for her as it does for me.

These kinds of moments are ripe with potential for conflict. They can become opportunities to implode, to let frustration boil over and to lay blame—to accuse your partner of not doing enough. But they are also opportunities to choose a different path, to take ownership of your feelings and handle the situation yourself, recognizing that the need is yours and yours alone. It is a moment for self-reflection, a chance to understand why the scene matters so much—to you—and to decide how you want to respond, not just for your sake, but for the sake of your family harmony.

For me, it starts with recognizing that I need the common areas free of my daughter's clutter. I take ownership of keeping those spaces clear. At the same time, I invest my energy into teaching her the value of tidiness, hoping it becomes something she appreciates as she grows.

But if I find myself overwhelmed and unable to keep up with this task, I do have the option of letting it go. I can choose not to let the stress consume me. Every scenario like this can be used as an opportunity for self-reflection, a chance to dive deeper into myself and question whether this value is truly worth holding on to or passing down to my child.

And whenever my partner steps in to help, even if it's in small or different ways than I might have hoped for, I can choose gratitude over resentment. I can appreciate her support, however it shows up, rather than feeling frustrated by what it might lack.

I chose this particular trigger and value because it's ever-present, always lingering at the forefront of my mind. But, of course, it's just one of many. We all have our triggers—each one a marker on the complex map of parenthood. Experiencing them is an inevitable part of this remarkable journey, a journey not just into the world of parenting but, more profoundly, into the depths of ourselves.

What this journey reveals about who you are offers a unique opportunity—to grow, evolve, and become a better version of yourself. It's an invitation to be a more understanding partner, a more present parent, and ultimately, a more complete human being.

## *Creating space for differences in parenting*

In the intricate dance of finding a partner, we're often advised to seek someone with similar values. It's sound advice, especially regarding shared beliefs and convictions on raising a child. Yet, without the actual experience, it's nearly impossible to fully understand what these values entail. Most of our ideas on raising children exist only at a surface level; it's not until we're in the thick of parenting that these ideas and values truly reveal themselves. This is why parents can act or say something that makes them pause, suddenly realizing that in that moment, they are embodying their own parent. Before they know it, they're recreating a scene from their own childhood—and it's startling. This unveiling is one of the more beautiful experiences of the parenting journey, showing us deeper layers of ourselves that we might have never known were there.

However, challenges arise when these revelations conflict with our partner's unveiled views and parenting style. For instance, my partner and I knew from the start that hitting our child wasn't an option, but we never anticipated that our approach to feeding her would be a point of contention. Similarly, while we'd agreed that religion wouldn't be introduced at a young age, we later discovered contrasting beliefs on celebrating holidays. Speaking of holidays, things shifted significantly after we became parents. Before, we both saw holidays as ploys by a capitalist system—a convenient way to drain bank accounts throughout the year. We felt aligned in our stance against succumbing to what we viewed as a commercialized "machine." But once our daughter arrived, mom softened, wanting our child to experience the same magic she remembered from her own childhood holidays. I, however, didn't have many magical holiday memories, so it took me some time to meet her where she was. I was still very much focused on what I saw as needless spending.

I share these experiences to offer this advice: allow space for your partner's parenting style, especially if this is their first time as a parent. Parenting reveals parts of ourselves that often surprise us. It allows us to make necessary adjustments to become better parents and evolve into the higher versions of ourselves we aspire to be. Allowing space for your partner's approach means releasing judgment and criticism and replacing them with curiosity. This process is also an opportunity to deepen your understanding of the person you're sharing this journey with. Remember, you are two people who were raised in different households and shaped by unique experiences. No matter how similar your backgrounds may seem, there will always be differences. Approach these differences with clear eyes, an open mind, and a desire to grow closer and become better, both as individuals and as a team. If you do, the results will be a stronger, more unified partnership, no matter what challenges come your way.

# CHAPTER 12

# Peeping Out of the Window

*"Be here now"*

– **Ram Dass**

A few years ago, I found myself in a job that I genuinely enjoyed. The work was simple, almost mindless—tasks I could perform without much mental strain. This left me plenty of time to doom-scroll on the internet, float between being a social butterfly or a recluse, and gossiping with some of the best co-workers about others while being paid more than the job warranted. Not a bad gig, right? Yet, there was that big window in my office and a clock on the adjacent wall. Every morning, I'd watch the sun slowly break through the clouds, and by the time I packed up to leave, it would be setting. In those in-between hours, I spent more time than I'd care to admit just watching the world go by.

I'd been staring out of such windows for most of my career—whether I was doing close to nothing or grinding through quotas and piles of documents. The job itself wasn't necessarily depressing; it was the reality that every tick of the clock was one less second I had to be part of the world beyond that window, the world where the real "party" seemed to be—the journeys and experiences I wanted for my life.

I approached those jobs the same way I approached relationships with the child I desperately wished to bring into this world always in mind. I nailed those interviews the same way I presented myself to my partner—as someone worthy of fathering her child. I was ecstatic when I got hired, just as I was when my daughter was finally born. But neither excitement nor achievement erased the feeling of looking out through those large windows, longing for something more.

## The Window of Parenthood

Parenthood can often feel like the most demanding of all jobs. The workload is immense, and there are few genuine breaks. When you're stationed in parenthood, especially while transitioning into it fully, the "window" becomes a reflection—showing you who you used to be, what you used to do before you had children, what you hope to do again when they are older or out of the house, and what everyone else, seemingly "free," is doing right now.

I've always been a traveler at heart who thrives on being on the move. But when a child comes along, the "going" gets tough. Gone are the spontaneous days of jumping on a plane with just a backpack. Now, there are extra tickets to buy, larger rooms to book, the logistical feat of moving everyone from point A to point B on time, and all the emotional and physical baggage that comes with it. To save money and hassle, I often stay home, gazing into a different kind of window—my phone screen—where, with just a flip of my thumb, I can see friend after friend having a blast in another country, living rich experiences. I use that same thumb to "heart" their status, all while waiting and wishing for my turn to be on the other side again.

Then, there are moments when my daughter poops on the carpet after I just asked her if she needed to go and she insisted she didn't, or climbs on the furniture yelling, "Look at me, Daddy!" after I've told her not to a dozen times, or simply walks up to me with her eyes closed and lips puckered for a kiss. In those moments, it dawns on me just how remarkably forgettable all those experiences on the other side of the window truly are and how deeply I'll miss these moments with her as she grows older. At this stage in my parenting journey, I can honestly say I sometimes enjoyed life without children more. But I can also say that some of my life's sweetest, most irreplaceable moments would never have existed without my little girl.

You had a life before having a child, and perhaps it was more carefree, more enjoyable. There's nothing wrong with looking out that window and feeling what you feel. In fact, I'd argue it's healthy to allow yourself those thoughts without beating yourself up with judgment. But the reality remains: that life is a thing of the past, and resisting the life you have now will only make it harder to exist in—and even harder to enjoy.

## *Dreams Deferred*

My father always believed a man should provide. From a young age, he sent me into the fields to pick produce from dawn to dusk, taking half the money I earned. "Once you're married, your money belongs to your family," he'd say. One day, he led me to an old dresser in his barn, pulled out the smallest drawer, and said, "This is the only space I have in the house. And look at it—half of that is taken up by your mother." I remember this moment vividly because it was the first time I felt a twinge of fear about marriage. There were countless small moments like this—little ways he conveyed that a man must sacrifice himself to have a family. I got the message, but I fear he sacrificed too much.

Unlike me, my father always wanted children; it was his greatest desire. After having my own, it's hard for me to fully understand it, but that's what he wanted. Unfortunately, my mother couldn't give him that. They didn't discuss it much, but through my childhood snooping, I discovered my mom could never carry a pregnancy to term. Once they accepted this reality, they chose to adopt, which is how I came into the family. To this day, I have mixed feelings about it. As much as I appreciate him for choosing to be my father, I wish he had given himself the gift of having his own.

As a lover, husband, and man with dreams, I can imagine the inner turmoil he faced at those crossroads. One path would lead to having his own biological children but destroy the life he had built with my mother; the other would mean raising another man's child, and perhaps always wondering, *"What if?"*

He never talks about it, but I know it's there. He's been a good father, but I can feel the resentment—not toward me, but toward my mother, for not being able to give him what he wanted most. And more so, toward himself for not granting that desire to himself. I've never felt the closeness between them that you'd expect from a couple who chose to walk this path together. I've seen companionship, partnership, and friendship, but rarely, if ever, the deep, loving bond I see in photos of them before I was born. My mother has loved my father since they were teenagers, but when his deepest dream died, a part of him vanished. I believe it left when he abandoned the part of himself that held that dream. From that point on, he decided to play the character he'd created rather than the man he truly wanted to be.

As men, we're told, taught, and expected to be responsible. But rarely are we truly prepared when the time comes. We make mistakes, sometimes sacrificing more of ourselves than is necessary. It reminds me of when I was so shaken by a food documentary that I gave up meat. Not knowing how to eat differently, I simply removed the meat and added more carbs. With no experience with vegetables, I essentially became a "Carbatarian." Eating became miserable, and the effects on my body were worse. I was tired and sluggish, and where I once had muscles, I now had sagging fat. It was a wholly unpleasant experience.

You can bear the weight of responsibility for your child without abandoning yourself. Sacrifices must be made, but if you have the opportunity to fulfill the deepest desire of your heart, perhaps it's worth going on the journey to give that gift to yourself rather than walking a path littered with "what ifs." When you abandon the part of yourself that holds your dream, a piece of you follows. It may even be the part that made your partner fall in love or made your children see you as something magical. You might feel increasingly distant from a version of yourself you cherished. I know my father knows he's in his last good years, and sometimes, I see him spiraling toward despair. I know what it would have meant for my mother and me if he had chosen to give himself his greatest desire, but it is my love for him that makes me wish he had.

Life often tells us "no" to the desires we hold. Even if we ignore that "no" and give ourselves the green light, the price may be steep. Perhaps, though, the price is worth it, especially if saying "no" comes with a penalty that we—and everyone close to us—must pay.

I'm not advocating for reckless abandonment or shirking responsibilities. What I'm advocating for is building a life from the truth of who you are so that the cost of carrying it is more than worth the strain. It's incredibly challenging to show up for a life that feels like it costs you the journey you deeply desire.

Sometimes, it's the process of building—or living in what we've built—that reveals hidden parts of ourselves. When that happens, you must decide what you'll do with that truth. The easiest thing to do is abandon what we've created, leaving everyone in the rubble. This path can lead to long-term suffering in the form of regret and despair. Instead, find a path to the journey you want in a way that offers a better version of yourself to those connected to you because that creates a better reality for everyone, including yourself.

You might exhaust yourself looking for a path with little pain, and that's okay—perhaps even commendable in some respects. But if you cannot find that path, don't let the pain stop you. Fear, too, is a mental trick that can create barriers between you and the version of yourself living your dream. The value of fear is that it stops us long enough to consider the consequences of moving forward. When moving forward makes sense, my mantra is: feel the fear and do it anyway.

So many men leave behind a valuable part of themselves because they think it's the "right" thing to do. But so much suffering comes from self-abandonment, and when this happens, everyone attached to that man pays the price.

## *A Lot of "I Gotta"*

One major transition in becoming a parent is shifting from spending your days and nights how you want to live with a perpetual, weighty list of things you have to do. I call it "a lotta, I gotta." This list is different for everyone. My dad used to refer to his as the "honey-do" list because that was how my mother's requests would typically begin: "Honey, do this," or "Honey, do that." There is an enormous amount of responsibility that comes with caring for a little one—it affects every aspect of your life.

For me, that list meant being home a lot more than I liked, buying boxes upon boxes of diapers and wipes, having wrenching conversations with my partner about our different parenting styles, and getting up every five minutes to cater to my child's endless needs. I swear I've never gotten up so many times in my life. A child is a monumental addition to your life and will inevitably affect your lifestyle. The real question is: How will you allow that change to affect you?

There was a time when you could go to sleep knowing that when you opened your eyes again, it would be morning. You could spend the entire day doing whatever you liked, moving seamlessly from one moment to the next, with a fair amount of control over your emotional and mental state. If you compare that life to this one, it's easy to fall into a hole of despair, longing for what used to be.

The reality is that the life-changing addition—a child—is here to stay. No matter how you feel about it, you signed yourself up for "18 to Life" the moment you decided to go down this road. To transition smoothly into this new chapter (and to enjoy it), you must change the way you think about it. When you change your thoughts, you change your life.

Accept that the journey of parenting is something happening for you, not to you. This journey will take you to the deepest parts of yourself in ways nothing else can or will. If you choose not to resist, parenting becomes a journey of becoming more patient, empathetic, nurturing, wise, loving, and understanding of yourself. It is a path that pushes you to ascend to a higher version of who you are.

Because of this, whether we are enjoying the journey or not, it can be incredibly tough to navigate. I've had several moments in this process where I felt like a broken man. In many of those moments, I wished I had never taken this path. But what always appeared through that brokenness was a light—a gift, a reward for embracing the journey. It is a revealed truth about myself.

When you find yourself broken, as you will on many occasions, and you uncover that hidden truth, the question is: What will you do with it? You should always use truth to build a reality that aligns with the best of what you envision yourself—as a parent, partner, and human being. When you find that you are not as patient as you thought, what will you do? When you realize you don't have all the answers, what then? And what about when something surfaces within you that horrifies others? When they act as your mirror, revealing this truth to you, will you be defensive and dismissive, or will you accept it and grow?

Sometimes, the window seems like the price to pay for being on this journey, but the real trouble isn't what's happening outside the window or even on the ride itself. What bothers you is how you perceive it all.

It takes no effort to focus on your life with a mindset of "I have to," because that's the reality if you want to maintain everything you've called into your own life. But the small shift of viewing it all as something you get to do changes everything. Note, I'm not saying it's easy. When my daughter is sitting right behind me while I'm driving, crying at the top of her lungs for reasons I can't comprehend, I'm not thinking, "Amazing! Look at how I get to spend the next 30 minutes of this drive." I'm actually quite pissed off. But I don't want to be. I don't want to feel upset; I don't want my day ruined, my nerves shot, or my daughter to remember me as a disgruntled father.

Changing to a "get to" mindset involves being curious about why she's exhibiting this behavior, learning how to be a responsive father at that moment, practicing the art of patience, and participating in the scene in such a way that it creates a memory my daughter can look back on with gratitude. I could complain about all the diapers I have to buy, or I could use these demands as motivation to find a way to increase my income so that the price of diapers becomes a non-issue. That doesn't have to mean working more hours in a soul-sucking 9-to-5; it could be just the push I needed to turn a passion into a source of income.

Changing how you perceive your responsibilities changes how you feel about them. You can view them as a burden, a task, a messed-up situation you've placed yourself into, a "job," or you can see them as something of a game—a challenge that you get to play, no matter how tough. It's the same issue but changing how you perceive it changes how you feel about it and, ultimately, how you live your life. It gives you a different energy when you contemplate your day.

If I'm sick of my job, my dread of getting up for work on Monday starts the moment I leave on Friday. But I always feel good about getting a chance to "play." And If you can't change the job, turn it into play.

## *Disappearing Friends*

On a recent trip back where I was raised, I took some time to walk through the now-condemned plot of land I once called home. We were raised in a small trailer with a large front yard, and on many afternoons, forty or so neighborhood kids could be found playing anything from red-light/green-light to flag football. Our neighbors were our family. My grandparents lived in the little purple house just behind us, and my favorite uncle was our neighbor to the right. Back then, if you needed a condiment, you didn't run to the store—you went next door. The same went for finding a babysitter; if my parents needed someone to watch us, it was as simple as finding an available family member or friend, and it was always free. This is something like what my dad envisions when he encourages me to have more children, especially with his "the more you have, the less expensive they are" speech. It's often said that it takes a village to raise a child. Times have changed, and much of our society has moved on from the village.

Unless you've managed to keep or create this dynamic, brace yourself: your friends and family may not be around much to help on this journey. The singles are too busy doing what people without children do—whatever they want, just like you did when you were in the same situation. Even the ones who are present won't have much to offer beyond the occasional visit, some babysitting, or advice that may or may not be useful. The ones who do have children are too busy managing their own lives to give much to you.

It's easy to take it personally—after all, they were the ones making all those promises at the baby shower. But don't. You'll see your single friends having a blast doing child-free things without you, and you may want to sulk in resentment. Don't. Your family may not play the part you envisioned when you imagined what life would be like, and you might feel the urge to resent them, too. Don't.

The ones who have made it to the other side of this journey are enjoying their time to themselves—surely, you can understand that. The ones who haven't walked the path you're on don't know any better; they simply can't relate to what you're going through. I sometimes cringe at the lack of awareness I had as a friend to those with children. I'd walk into my friend's homes, see them absolutely wrecked by toddlers, and ask, "So, how's it going?" as if we were still facing the small issues of college life. There was the time when a friend started sending me pictures of her child's poop on the floor during potty training. Then, I saw it as a clear violation of boundaries and, well, gross. But now, as I dread waking up to poop all over my daughter's room, I see clearly—she just needed to vent.

Again, don't take it personally and don't sulk in resentment. Just be sure to be a good friend when your friends bring their own bundle of pain into the world. I absolutely meant joy.

You will endure many hardships during this time, and you'll find yourself in moments where your last nerve is being trampled on. In all of that, I implore you to heed the advice of the elder passerby who has gone down this same path: find the magic in the storm and enjoy it. This journey is moving along like sand passing through your fingers, and before you know it, it'll be gone, and you'll be one of those passersby giving the same advice.

I am guilty of daydreaming of all the possibilities I could have had if I hadn't committed myself to "eighteen years to life." But then my daughter taps me on the nose, says, "Boop," opens that beautiful smile, and laughs. In that moment, I know I'm experiencing something magical—something that won't always be—and something I will one day shed tears over when remembering. In that moment, I know I am on my own amazing journey. That instantly rids me of the negative feelings I could be harboring. Rest assured, for better or worse, there is no experience you could be having that is more enriching.

## *Mindset and Suffering*

*People often think they are unhappy because of the circumstances in their lives. In most cases, they are unhappy because of what they are telling themselves about what is going on around them.*

*— Eckhart Tolle*

The suffering starts and ends with the mind. During my lowest points, I would wake up to relentless inner voices telling me how bad my life was and how foolish I was to put myself in this situation. It didn't take much to amplify these thoughts—a cry, a breakfast rejection, toys scattered all over the floor, realizing we'd run out of diapers—any of it could set off a chain of thoughts that would ultimately cause suffering. These thoughts were easy to accept, creating a comfortable bed for suffering to lie in. And that negative energy is something everyone in the home will feel. I didn't want anyone to feel what I was carrying, but it was inevitable; it always is. You can hide a lot from others, but you can't hide your energy from the people closest to you. They don't just know; they feel it.

## *Wishing time away*

I've been warned against it on several occasions, but when you're in the thick of the parts that you have a strong disdain for, it's much easier said than done. During this journey most of us will run into experiences that we wish we could hit a fast forward button on. I think I've shared quite a bit of mine throughout these pages and I'm sure you aren't having a hard time thinking up your own. It's nothing to feel ashamed of, there's a lot of life that a fast-forward button would be useful for. What I will tell you is you don't have to wish the time away, as it will be gone before you know it. And you will miss it. The moments that are grueling now will be the ones that you laugh about later, and the sweet ones that you enjoy during the same time will be the ones you will give anything to live in again. I don't miss the part where I slept only three hours a night for almost a year, but I do miss my little girl being that small, walking around with her riding my forearm and hand. The past is behind you, the future is uncertain, but the moment is now, and it's always what you make of it.

As I am writing today, my mother is in the hospital, nearing the point of fighting for her life. She's just a few days removed from an overdue brain surgery and she's having some complications. The first time I saw her post-op she was asleep with tubes and bandages all over. It was the first time I truly saw her as a mortal being who could take a last breath at any moment and break my heart. I've seen her awake since, and she was doing better, but my last call with her was frightening and eye-opening. Through tears and worry, she spoke to me like someone on their deathbed; it was so excruciating to listen to her. She said many things that touched my heart, and one thing she said that I immediately knew I had to write down. "I'm helpless" she cried out, "I can't cook, I can't clean, I can't do anything for any of the people who depend on me to take care of." What was so striking to me was this: what she wanted to do most, on what she believed could be her death bed, were the same things she had been complaining about having to do in every conversation we had over the past twenty years. It made me think about how much I've complained about what I have to do as a father and my thoughts if I were in her position.

Our culture is terrified of death, so much so that we've successfully hidden it from ourselves. We've found ways to tuck it into the crevasses of our society so that we can move throughout our days as though it doesn't exist. We go to sleep, we live, we wake up, and it seems we've deluded ourselves to the point where we expect this to go on forever. It only hits home when a loved one is fighting for their life or when they lose it; even then, it's only a few days before the reality of our existence wears away. And when we hear of others dying it's okay because death is something that only happens to others, not us. Maybe it's something we should allow ourselves to contemplate more, especially when we so badly want something hard to end. Perhaps it wouldn't be so difficult to exist in the hard times if you allow yourself to think about the fact that soon it will all end.

Just as death can be a reminder of that, so can life. Without a child, one can move through a lot of life, ignoring their mortality, but the changing face of a child reflects the truth whether one wishes to see it or not. They are getting older, and so are you. As fast as the scenery passes through the window of a moving train, so are the moments with your child as a little one. Sometimes, it can be hard to see it that way as they sure can make it hard, but to the best of your ability, remember that you are living in the time you will miss the most. Even the worst of it can become a part of the most cherished memories.

Instead of wishing time away, embrace it—the good, the bad, and the mundane. You are living through moments that are precious simply because they are finite. And that is the beauty and the curse of time—it slips away, whether we want it to or not.

## CHAPTER 13
# Everything Is Changing

*"The only way to make sense out of change is to plunge into it, move with it, and join the dance."*

– Alan Watts

I've always had a thing for nature, especially for a flourishing, brightly colored bloom. I've known this about myself for a long time, but I didn't fully grasp how much they meant to me until I first encountered the Chinese pagoda flower. A row of them was nestled in the backyard of the first home my partner and I visited as potential buyers. The house itself was smaller than I would have liked, and there were aspects that didn't appeal to me. But the diversity of flowers and plants in the yard drew me in like a moth to a flame. Yet, it was the row of pagodas that made me turn to my real estate agent and say, "Let's write up an offer. I'm sold."

These pagodas stood as tall as I did, with large, lush green leaves cascading from their slender trunks. Their trunks were lanky and flexible, allowing them to sway gracefully with the wind. Atop the trunks sat clusters of flowers the color of rich strawberry sorbet, triangular in form and delicate to the touch. The balance and beauty of the trees allowed them to dance with the wind and watching them do so gave me a sense of peace that I longed to settle down with.

After seeing them, I no longer cared how old the house was or how much work it would need. I just wanted to be near those flowers, to own a piece of the serenity they brought me. In retrospect, that's a whimsical reason to buy a house—especially when I could have just visited a local botanical garden and experienced them at my leisure. But I had to own them, and because of that, I had to pay the price of watching them die.

This is true of anything that enchants us to the point where we feel we must have it; at some point, we must mourn the cost of it, the effort required to maintain it, and the inevitable loss of it. This was one of those lessons I couldn't wait to teach my daughter. Blooms also caught her eyes, and she'd always insist on having them. With a quick sweep of her hand and a tug, every flower that enchanted her would be hers, only for her to eventually watch its vibrance fade away. On one occasion, she angrily threw a flower onto the ground because it wasn't "doing the thing"—the thing, in this case, being 'staying pretty.' I told her that the flower changed because she changed the nature of its existence. It's a lesson we all learn as children, yet many of us struggle to carry gracefully into adulthood. We grant ourselves a desire and then look as lost as a four-year-old holding a withered flower when things inevitably change.

Enchantment is often the bait that lures us into plucking something, only to watch what we've plucked change in our hands. When you "pluck" your partner, you must watch the version of them that you fell in love with evolve and sometimes fade. When you "pluck" a life with a child, you must say goodbye to the version of your life without children. When you "pluck" a life completely different from the one you have, you must watch that former version of yourself slip away as well.

This is a reality to consider carefully before picking anything—a reality you should prepare yourself for.

Many will fight against change in a relationship, especially when they have committed themselves to something they were initially enchanted by. However, as the only constant in life, change should be the greatest expectation. Imagine being something that changes yet demanding that nothing else does. It doesn't stand to reason and becomes the basis for many arguments, resentments, and often heartbreaks. When you build your family, so much of your life changes. The more you uproot yourself to build a new life, the more of your old self you leave behind. We are responsible for being mindful of what we choose to bring into our lives; many things may require us to plant deeper roots to sustain what we've acquired.

For me, a new house required more money, which required more work. A partner required more of me emotionally than I had ever given before, so I had to connect myself to something that could nourish me in return. And a first child required more than I ever imagined I'd have to give. I wasn't prepared for that, and I had to pay the price in some of the most excruciating ways to meet her needs. When you build a family, change is happening everywhere, and you can either resent your partner and yourself for it or you can learn to flow with the change that is inevitable, not only in your life but within you.

These changes add pressure and stress that many of us are simply not prepared for—and couldn't be without experiencing them firsthand. My father did everything he could to prepare me for partnership as he knew it, but even that wasn't nearly enough.

## The Cost of Enchantment

We bought that home in the fall of the year Dahlia was born. The reality of what I had done to myself began to settle in when winter arrived. I felt a profound sadness as I watched my precious pagodas wither away in the cold. My frustration grew when I realized how much work awaited me inside that house. Dahlia was conceived in the spring of that year, and by the time we were in the throes of new parenthood, the dream home had turned into something of a nightmare. All the plants around the house had browned or died, the house was falling apart, my partner's mental health was fragile from postpartum depression, the baby's crying was driving us both mad, and I was at a total loss, scrambling to keep everything together.

If you find yourself in a similar situation, a few things can help you through. First, understand that "keeping everything together" can often be the problem. The more you give yourself, the more weight you place on your shoulders. Sometimes, it's necessary to remove some of that weight, whether by offloading it entirely or by sharing the burdens with capable members of your family. Men are often taught to carry as much burden as possible so their family members can move freely, but not only is this disabling for the family, it robs men of quality time with their loved ones. It contributes to why we often end up in the grave earlier.

Secondly, remember that you're not the only one under pressure. We made agreements when my partner and I decided to have a child. She looked me in the eyes and said she wanted to make our house a home and keep it that way, and I committed to taking care of everything else. For me, this was the perfect scenario. It was easy when it was just the two of us;

it became an overwhelming full-time job once the baby arrived. In such situations, it's easy to focus on your burdens while dismissing what your partner is going through, especially if you feel your load is heavier. No matter what another person is facing, you can never fully understand how heavy it is for them—just as you can't hand someone a barbell and expect it to feel the same to them as it does to you. You have to listen to and trust the person you're sharing this responsibility with, and hopefully, you've chosen someone who can offer you the same trust and understanding.

Thirdly, keep in mind that your family feels and is affected by your presence and energy. If you are weighed down, stressed, frustrated, or depressed, your family feels it. You can sit in your car to gather a good face before walking in and pretend everything is alright, but they will know and feel the truth. Not only will your energy be sensed, but what you are going through will seep into your interactions, and before you know it, you may find yourself destroying the scenes you once desired and creating those you will regret.

### *Finding Your Well*

Finally, you have to plug yourself into what you need to fill yourself so that you can provide what your family needs from you. It wasn't until I found myself depleted by the rigors of day-and-night parenting that I realized how much I'd uprooted myself from fertile soils. Connections with close friends faded, and we moved away from the place that felt most like home. In that move, I gave up something valuable: close proximity to the beach. Since I was a teenager, the expansive waters and light sands have been a place of refuge and recharge. I love the beach because it loves me in a way that is hard to find elsewhere; it gives so much without asking for anything in return.

You need something or someone like this in your life—a well you can draw from that isn't drained by you and requires nothing from you in return. As a father who wishes to give his best, much will be required of you. You need your own beach or row of pagodas—something that fills you simply by its existence. There may come a time when you need arms you can relax into and weep. Making space for something just for you is the gift you'll need to show up as the best version of yourself—or, at the very least, to stave away the worst.

Taking on a responsibility for something, be it a home, a relationship, or even a dream, comes with a cost. It demands care, commitment, and acceptance of change. But when you understand that everything is transient—every bloom, every moment, every stage—you begin to see the true beauty of it all. You learn to cherish the dance with the wind and to let go when the time comes, knowing that life is a series of enchanted moments, each as fleeting as the last.

# CHAPTER 14

# The Perfect Moment

*"There is nothing more precious than being in the present moment. Fully alive, fully aware."*

– Thích Nhất Hạnh

One of the longest days of early parenting for me was filled with blowout diapers, temper tantrums, food scattered all over the floor, and every other energy-draining event that Dahlia could possibly throw my way. By the time her bedtime came around, my nerves were so frayed that I was running on fumes, barely holding it together as I navigated our evening routine. I was in my head for most of it, ruminating over why I had chosen this path for myself, wishing I could fast-forward just enough to collapse onto my own bed. Even rocking her to sleep felt like a chore. I held her in my arms, sang nursery rhymes, and made soft, wind-like sounds for what felt like an eternity. I remember the frustration bubbling inside me as her eyes remained wide open, staring into mine, seemingly challenging me to stay present. I held her until my arms and back trembled with exhaustion. I shifted her so her head could rest on my shoulder and sat down to rock her in the chair. Not long after, she finally drifted off to sleep.

Relief washed over me—a mix of accomplishment and the sweet sensation of her gentle snores vibrating against my chest.

I took a deep breath, exhaled, and allowed my body to relax for the first time since I woke up that morning. But the moment I did that—and I mean the exact moment—Dahlia released a heaping amount of semi-digested formula all over me.

It started with a sound that could have been a hiccup, but the next thing I knew, I felt the warm, wet sensation of her vomit running down my shoulder and chest. It was so sudden that I nearly jumped out of the chair. At that moment, I felt an upending explosion inside me, ready to go off. Whatever reserves of patience and energy I had managed to cling to throughout the day had finally run dry. I wanted to put her in her crib and walk away. I wanted to cry. I wanted to be mad at something—anything—or even at myself. I wanted to throw something at the wall, to feel the fullness of the rage building within me.

But instead, I laughed. It wasn't a belly laugh or a cackle, but something in between—a sound that came up from deep within, both desperate and liberating. It was exactly what I needed.

It may seem like the most irrational response, but it was perfect, given how I felt inside. When I thought about the entire day and how it had culminated in a cascade of vomit, I realized it couldn't have been a more fitting setup for a total meltdown. That irony made it hilarious. It was like a scene from a comedy movie, the kind where everything that could go wrong does, and it becomes so absurd that it's funny. It's the kind of joke that everyone in the audience laughs at because they've been there in some way or another.

I'm sharing this moment with you to let you know that when you feel like you're on the verge of losing control, you also have the choice to see it all for the cosmic joke that it is and have a good laugh about it. You can use that moment to reflect on how you're being affected and why you're allowing yourself to feel that way.

We tend to think of perfect moments as those where the universe seems to have conspired to bring us pure joy. But it's just as perfect when everything comes together to deliver a moment that feels like the opposite of joy. In both instances, you are given the gift of a timely and clear mirror.

Perhaps the greater gift comes when the moment brings pain, frustration, or even despair. Because that is when you are truly open to yourself, these moments show you your triggers, fears, and limitations. They reflect parts of yourself that might be hidden, giving you a starting point on a path toward who you wish to become. While the situation itself might not be funny, the way life packages these experiences and presents them to you can be. You look at life and say, "Yeah, you got me this time."

As Dr. Wayne Dyer often said, "When you change the way you view an experience, the experience changes." Realizing that I could have been brought to my knees by the events of that day inspired me to reevaluate how I had internalized each moment. I only reached that point of frustration because of how I chose to receive and react to each situation. Had I seen every challenge as the gift it was, that "perfect moment" at the end of the day would have felt entirely different. Instead of rage, I might have felt some semblance of joy—even with half-digested formula trickling down my back.

*Well, maybe.*

Back then, I couldn't wait to put her down so I could escape to myself. But today, I can only hold my daughter in my arms for a fraction of the time, and soon, it will no longer be possible at all. Back then, I was desperate for her to close her eyes and fall asleep. Today, getting her to lock eyes with me the way she used to might require a bribe of something sweet, and only for a few seconds. Whether we allow ourselves to feel the fullness of these moments as they happen or much later in life, they are all sweet in their own way. They are all perfect because they reveal hidden parts of us to ourselves.

Moments are our mirrors, and so are the comings and goings of the daily events in our lives. When peace finds you, it is as sweet as the chaos that preceded it. When life comes together in a way that makes everything else disappear except the moment itself, you will discover parts of yourself that have been tucked away in the deepest spaces. Catch yourself in those perfect moments and give yourself the time to make more of them—something wonderful for yourself. Whether pleasant or not, they can all be used to move closer to the highest version of yourself.

### *The Mirror of Parenthood*

The desire to have children has always fascinated me. Why would anyone willingly choose such a path? There is so much pain and anguish involved, along with risk, uncertainty, and unbelievable sacrifice, for what often seems like very little in return. To this day, I've given my child more than she could ever know, and yet, her favorite word upon any request that doesn't involve immediate pleasure is "no." Frustrating, to say the least. So, why do we put ourselves through this? I think there are countless reasons—the biological pull to procreate, the desire to have someone to truly love, the wish to see oneself combined with a partner in form. The list is endless, filled with both noble and flawed reasons to bring a child into the world. But all those reasons point to one thing: a mirror.

Parenthood is the greatest journey one can embark on to get the clearest look at oneself. The true reward of this journey is not the child itself but the clear reflection of yourself that comes with it. This reflection offers you the chance to grow into a better version of yourself, should you accept the challenge. When I told my father that I did not remember much of my toddlerhood, he smiled and said, "It wasn't for you to remember." He was right; it was for him.

Many of the frustrations a parent experiences with their child have little to do with the child and everything to do with what the child is reflecting back to them. Your triggers, traumas, fears, limitations, anxieties, and insecurities are placed in front of you. Because you cannot run from the responsibility of caring for the child, you cannot run away from looking at yourself. Even if you try to escape that responsibility, you're only forced to see yourself even more deeply.

When we are unable to enjoy our children, it is often because we are unable to enjoy ourselves. We've grown up, forgotten how to turn everything into play—a skill we were born with. We've learned how to suffer, how to bury our traumas and wounds, how to strand the child within. The world told us we had to be serious, and we bent to its will. For all those reasons, the relationship with our child suffers greatly.

I once heard someone give this advice: "Let them make their mess, let them make their noise, and let them jump on the sofa because one day they will be gone, and that will be what you miss the most."

It sounded poetic, but I was also a bit triggered by the "let them jump on the sofa" part because I get triggered by my daughter jumping on the sofa. When she does it, I feel anger well up inside. I've been telling her to stop since the first time she dove onto the sofa in perfect Superman form. Of course, she tests that boundary every chance she gets, along with my nerves. One day, I wondered why it was such a trigger for me. It's harmless; she's having fun, and the couch is only a few years away from the dump anyway. Why not let her enjoy it? I posed the question to my followers on social media, and the first question I was asked was, "Were you allowed to jump on the sofa when you were a kid?"

I don't know the answer to this question, as time has seemingly stripped most of my childhood memories from my reach, but I'm certain there's no way my parents would have allowed it. And I'm sure that after the third time, I would have been met with a hand, a belt, or a switch.

Now the question becomes, am I denying her that happiness because it was denied to me? Am I feeling rage when she does it because I am traumatized by the rage my parents felt when I did it? I believe so. With that realization, I can choose to allow my child a little more happiness by letting her jump on the sofa.

To be perfectly honest, I still don't allow it, though. Like most others, I tend to fall short of following my own advice, no matter how sound it is. But here, the advice is to explore within yourself the reasons behind denying your child any form of happiness. It is always connected to something, and releasing yourself from whatever hold it has on you will open a channel that flows through you to your child. This channel becomes a passageway for happiness to flow freely, for both of you to enjoy, and for your connection to grow stronger. Your children show you your blockages and give you a chance to return to the version of yourself who could truly enjoy not only life but yourself.

## *Resist or play*

What an amazing journey we get to be taken on, with one catch: it requires us to allow it to be. It requires us to flow with the experiences of ourselves that our children open us to. That same journey can be absolute hell when we choose a path of resistance. Parenting will either soften or harden you, and it's not the child who gets the credit or the blame—it's always you. It all comes down to whether you choose to wrestle with the experience or play with it. There will always be tough times—perhaps even somewhere you find yourself questioning why you chose this journey for yourself—and that's okay. The job is so big that there has to be room for such thoughts and feelings, and for grace. Remember, no matter how stuck you feel in that space, you can always find your way back to an enjoyable experience by allowing yourself to play.

# Afterword shorts

The difference between this book and the others I wrote is that I could go on forever. There probably hasn't been a day that passed by without something happening that made me think, *I could add that to the book...* that's just how much of an adventure this ride really is. Of course, I can't add everything I'd like, this book has got to hit the shelves at some point. But I have collected some additional thoughts, lessons, and stories that I thought I'd share to close this book out.

## *Can I...?*

One of the most exhausting yet oddly enlightening things about raising a little one is the sheer persistence with which they ask for things. At three and a half years old, my child has already perfected the art of making demands, and it feels like a relentless hammer pounding against my patience every time a sentence starts with, "Can I...?" It's a refrain that echoes in my mind, pushing me to the brink of exasperation. Sometimes, I can't help but wonder if the universe, God, or whatever higher power we turn to for our needs feels a similar annoyance. Are we all, in some way, like nestlings with our mouths open to the sky, endlessly chirping for more, more, more?

But then, a realization dawned on me—one that shifted my perspective. Once I understood what I am to her—a source of security, comfort, and sustenance—the incessant requests became much more tolerable, even meaningful. She doesn't ask out of greed or malice; she asks because, in her little world, I am the provider of all things good and necessary. And in this simple, primal need, there is a lesson for me, too.

In recognizing my role as a provider for her, I began to see a reflection of my own constant inner demands and desires. The experience has become a mirror, teaching me to confront the wanting nature of my own self. Instead of becoming frustrated, I found a strange sense of gratitude for these moments. They have taught me to be more patient and to temper my own cravings for more—be it for time, success, or material comforts. Perhaps, in quieting her little wants, I am also learning to calm myself, finding peace in fulfilling needs rather than succumbing to endless desires. And so, what started as a hammer to my head has slowly transformed into a quiet rhythm, a dance between giving and receiving, between her growth and my own.

## *Gift*

Watching children grow up places us face to face with a reality that many of us prefer to ignore: time is slipping away. Every new milestone they reach—the first steps, the first words, the first day of school—reminds us that time is marching on, not just for them but for us as well. We feel the breath of our own mortality on the backs of our necks as we watch them leap from one phase of development to the next, seemingly faster with each passing year. With every growth spurt they have, we become more acutely aware of our own aging, of the wrinkles deepening on our faces and the gray hairs sprouting on our heads.

Yet, there's an unexpected gift that comes with embracing this inevitability. In accepting the fate that awaits us all, we are offered a precious opportunity: the chance to be fully present in the now. It's a sobering thought but a liberating one, too. Knowing that our time is finite can help us cherish the moments we have and lean into the present with all the love and attention we can muster. And in truth, this is what our children want more than anything from us—not the distractions of future planning or the regrets of what we could have done better, but the simplicity of our presence, here and now.

Children have an innate ability to exist fully in the present. They don't worry about what comes next; they don't dwell on what has already passed. They live in the moment, and in doing so, they remind us of a way of being that many of us have forgotten. When we manage to put down our phones, set aside our to-do lists, and really engage with them—whether it's playing on the floor, reading a bedtime story, or just listening to their endless questions—we are granted a glimpse into a life unburdened by the weight of the past and the future.

The moments when we can truly give ourselves to our children, when we can meet them in their world and share in their sense of wonder and discovery, will likely be the moments we look back on with the most fondness. It won't be the days when we were too busy to notice them growing up or too distracted to care. It will be those simple, passing instances when we were fully present, when we let go of the ticking clock of life and allowed ourselves to just be alongside them.

So yes, watching them grow is a reminder of our own aging and eventual departure. But in that reminder lies a beautiful truth: that the most profound gift we can give—to them and to ourselves—is our presence, undivided and complete. And maybe, in doing so, we learn to make peace with time, finding contentment in the here and now.

## *No*

I couldn't wait for my daughter to start speaking, not just because I was eager for the crying to stop, but because I had been anxious to truly meet her from the moment she was born. I wanted to meet her as a person—with her own thoughts, ideas, interpretations of reality, and unique expressions. I longed to see the world through her fresh, unfiltered eyes. And when the words finally came, they arrived with the promise of a deeper connection, a window into who she is and who she is becoming.

But as her vocabulary grew, I realized that who I would actually be meeting was a version of myself, reflected back through her. She is, after all, part of me—someone I willed into existence. This realization struck me hardest the first time she responded to me with a firm, unyielding "no." My father had warned me about the time when "no" would become a constant refrain, and I'd laughed it off, thinking I'd be prepared. But when it finally came, it stung in a way I didn't expect. It wasn't the "no" itself that hurt—it was the way she said it. Even the simplest, most innocent "no" came off as a sort of rebuke—quick, sharp, and blistering, as if she knew exactly how it would be received and delivered with precision.

Then, one day, as I was saying "no" to her, I heard it—the same tone, the same sharpness. Suddenly, I was transported back to those moments when she was smaller, and I would say "no" to her with a bit of amusement, almost entertained by how upset she would become. I remember a friend of mine watching these interactions and telling me, "Just wait until she's doing that to you." That same friend had also warned me that once Dahlia started walking, I'd never stop running. She was right about both.

Growing up, it was clear to me that there was a stark divide between adults and children—a divide reinforced by rules and, sometimes, punishment. Mirroring the behavior of adults, especially in a way that seemed defiant or challenging, was not tolerated. A child's "no" could be met with swift, sometimes painful consequences. Adults rarely take kindly to having their behavior mirrored back to them, especially when it highlights something unpleasant or comes from someone with less power, like a child. In many traditional parent-child dynamics, this imbalance of power means that respect often flows in one direction, with little room for dialogue or mutual understanding.

But in my journey as a parent, I've come to see things differently. When you allow your child the freedom of expression, you allow them to be a mirror, reflecting back to you everything you've taught them—consciously or unconsciously. If you ever find yourself unsure of how to treat your child, start treating them how you would want to be treated. Resist the instinct to shut them down or punish them for behaviors that are, in many ways, reflections of your own. Instead, when you are faced with something reflected back to you that you don't like, use it as an opportunity to change, to grow, and to model a better way.

It's easy to forget that our children are constantly offering us a roadmap to a better version of ourselves, one step at a time. They hold up a mirror to our habits, our words, our tones, and our actions. And if we're willing to look, really look, we might just find in that reflection the opportunity to become the parents—and the people—we aspire to be.

## *Grateful*

If I may return to the insatiable wanting nature of children, especially little ones, there is something else to keep in mind that may ease the irritation of your little one tugging on your shirt, desire gleaming in their eyes: it only gets worse from here, so enjoy it. That may not sound particularly comforting, but when you consider what they'll be asking for when they're older, well, you get it.

Every day, somewhere in the middle of the afternoon, I prepare the smoothie I had gone to bed dreaming about the night before. It's simple but perfect: a blend of chocolate protein powder, peanut butter powder, a bit of frozen banana, some avocado, crushed ice, almond milk, and just a touch of cinnamon. If you're a chocolate lover, it's pure heaven. My daughter agrees wholeheartedly. The moment the blender roars to life, I can hear her little feet tapping on the floor as she races over to me, her face lighting up with excitement. "Daddy, I love smoodies!" she exclaims. No, that's not a mistake—that's her adorable way of saying 'smoothies.'

For a while, I'd feel a pang of deflation every time she asked for some. I'd think, "I give this girl everything I have; can I just have this one thing to myself?" It seemed like a fair question, and it's one we often ask ourselves in many relationships—this desire for a moment of selfish pleasure. But everything changed when I realized that this wasn't just a one-way transaction. She was offering me something in return—a chance to see her light up with pure, unfiltered joy.

I used to say, "No, this is for Daddy," and she'd drop her little shoulders, her face falling into a pouty "Aww." I'd wrestle with the guilt of not giving her any, holding out until I was down to just a corner at the bottom of the cup. Then, I'd call her over and offer it to her. She'd turn that cup skyward and savor every last drop, her eyes closing with bliss. Usually, I'd shift my focus elsewhere while she drank, but one day, I decided to just watch her. She was unbelievably happy—ecstatic, even—for just the bottom corner of what was once a full 16-ounce smoothie.

I realized then how incredibly easy it was to make her happy. And I also realized that this, too, wouldn't last forever. Today, it's the corner of a cup; in a few short years, it could be a car—and probably not just any car.

Sometimes, we need to adjust our vision to see the beauty in what seems simple so that the experience becomes one of joy rather than one we perceive as burdensome. There is always a "last time" for something, but we often don't recognize it until we look back and see it has already come and gone. One day, I will offer my daughter the corner of a cup of smoothie, and she will take a few steps back and insist on more. That will be the moment I mourn all the times when just a corner could fill her with so much happiness.

It is wise to recognize in advance what you will mourn before the day arrives when you have no choice but to do so. To cherish these small moments now, while they're still happening, is to hold onto a piece of that joy, so that when the day comes that it's no longer enough, you can say you fully lived in those precious moments, savoring every drop, just like she did.

## *Reflection*

My daughter, just an infant at the time, and I were sitting at the table for dessert. For the first time, we were going to eat solid food together—strawberries. This moment felt profound to me. Here I was, sharing a small, yet significant experience with a little person who, not too long ago, was merely a thought in my mind and a desire in my heart.

I picked up a strawberry and extended it toward her. She reached out, her tiny fingers stretching with all their might but missing the fruit by the smallest margin. The distance must have been a mere centimeter, but to my surprise, that tiny gap set off a full-blown tantrum. It made no sense to me. I was so caught off guard, so bewildered by this unexpected eruption of emotion, that it felt as though my brain had short-circuited. I sat there, frozen, like a computer with a fried motherboard, unable to process or react. All I could do was sit there and watch as my daughter completely lost it over a strawberry that was so clearly within her reach.

So, I watched her. I watched her flail, cry, and exhaust herself until her wails dwindled to whimpers. In that quiet moment, it felt like my own system was rebooting. I found myself asking, "Are you done?"

And that's when it hit me—a sudden, almost haunting realization. I wasn't just hearing my own voice when asking her that question; I was hearing my father's voice, too. I could clearly recall him asking me the same question: "Are you done?" And in that instant, I realized I wasn't just looking at my child. I was looking at my father, at myself, and at a cycle that had been handed down through generations—a cycle of shutting down in the face of overwhelming emotions that felt irrational or disproportionate. I saw myself mirroring my father's very reaction, the same way his father likely did before him.

The words "Are you done?" felt heavy, almost painful to say because I remembered how much they hurt to hear as a child. Those words felt dismissive, as though my feelings didn't matter. It was a wound I didn't want to pass on to my daughter. I'm not sharing this to claim that I have evolved into the parent I want my daughter to have. I'm still very much a work in progress. But I want to share this with those who might find themselves in a similar moment of reflection and realization.

Try to see yourself and the world through the eyes of your child and to do so as often as possible. It's challenging because, from the vantage point of an adult, the child's reasoning can seem absurd, almost comical. But for them, that moment may be the hardest thing they've ever faced in their brand-new life. I have been through so much in my life, so through my eyes, missing a strawberry by a centimeter isn't a big deal. But to a one-year-old that could easily be the most disappointment they'd ever felt in their life. When it comes to parenting, so much makes sense when you see the world through the child.

Lastly, don't beat yourselves up over the emotional tools you may not yet have developed. Your child is your greatest mirror. Even if you believed you were supremely prepared for this job, that mirror will always reflect something you need to see and your attention. That reflection is an opportunity to heal and grow, not only for your "little you" but for yourself and everyone connected to you.

## *Clean up*

At the end of the day, the entire house is a whirlwind of chaos, evidenced by the ten or so messes that Dahlia has enthusiastically created throughout the day. She moves from one area to the next, leaving behind a trail of toys, books, and bits and pieces of her vivid imagination, turning each corner of our home into a testament of her joyful exploration. And after a long day, when exhaustion weighs heavy on our shoulders, we're left to pick up the remnants of her fun. One evening, I found myself sinking into the couch, surveying the cluttered landscape around me. The toys, the crumbs, the art supplies scattered like confetti. For a moment, I couldn't help but draw a parallel to my own life, thinking of all the messes I've made over the years that still need tidying up.

It hit me then, with a kind of weary amusement: aren't we all just big kids making bigger messes? We spill our emotions, scatter our unresolved issues, and drop the burdens of our own lives here and there, often expecting someone else to come along and clean them up. It was a sobering thought that shifted my perspective from frustration to a deeper understanding of the human condition. I realized that if I wanted Dahlia to grow into an adult who is aware of the messes she creates in her own life—both literally and metaphorically—we needed to start now.

So, we began to focus our energy on a new practice: having Dahlia clean up before moving on to her next adventure. "Before you leave this room," we tell her, "everything goes back where it belongs." It's a simple rule but a meaningful one. I believe it's crucial for children to learn the value of cleaning up their own messes early on. This isn't just about tidying up toys; it's about teaching them to recognize the impact of their actions and to take responsibility for them. It's about raising someone who won't wander through life unaware of the chaos they leave in their wake, expecting others to sweep in and fix it for them—especially not their parents.

I think I can speak for most of us when I say that we hope to someday retire from the role of cleaning up other people's messes. We want our children to grow into adults who can face the clutter they cause with accountability and care. And maybe, as they learn to pick up after themselves, we, too, can find the courage to clean up the lingering messes of our own lives, one small step at a time.

## *Promises*

I'm sitting on a two-thousand-dollar sofa that we only have because of the way my partner's eyes lit up when she first saw it. Looking through a large window of a home that I only bought because she said it was the one of her dreams. Through that window, I watched as the wind pushed mounds of snow from trees that the winter had left bare.

It felt amazing in the moment to give her heart's desire, but at this moment I laid as depressed as the sky was grey.

Six years prior to that scene I'd visited a white sanded beach called Siesta Key in Sarasota, Florida. I remember laying in the sand, being lightly cooked by sun and massaged by the wind; listening to the creeping waves and thinking, this is my home. One year later I was living there. I was on the other side of a marriage that I felt my soul was dying in and a cold-weather climate I promised myself I would never claim another address in.

I was finding myself, and I was happy for the first time in a while. I had little financial responsibilities, I was completely free, I was enjoying my new life and I made promises to myself that I would never put myself in the same situations again. I only needed one more thing to make my life complete—a child.

Funny how *just one more thing* can be what blows your entire life up. It's like a land mine buried in a beautiful prairie, except you survive the blast and what's left for you to make the best out of doesn't seem like much to work with. For many of us, a daunting task.

Over the course of the next four years I made a series of decisions that put me in the scene where we started, and many of those decisions involved breaking the promises that I made to myself.

Throughout our lives we all receive the messages that to be considered good we must sacrifice; this is especially true as a parent. I watched my grandfather sacrifice, my father, too. And from an early age my father pressed onto me that as a man it is essential that I am prepared and willing to sacrifice everything for the happiness of my family. And so, I did.

I gave my partner what she desired for her happiness and my daughter the same. I watched them enjoy these things, and seeing their joy fulfilled me in a way. But I would still feel an emptiness inside. When I would feel that emptiness, I'd close my eyes and see myself sitting at the edge of a bench, alone with my head bowed in sadness. It's a picture that lets me know how I abandoned an important part of myself, one broken promise at a time.

My advice to you, father, is to forego the experience of abandoning yourself. Even for your family. In giving your family everything they desire you risk the chance of everyone losing you, and that includes yourself. When you do that you don't get appreciation in return, you get resentment, and then you begin to give it in return. Angry at everyone for not being grateful for your sacrifice, before turning that anger onto yourself for sacrificing what you never needed to.

As I discussed in the first "What She Taught Me," once you find the direction for your life you must build it with conviction. Always be open to good advice, but do not cast your inner compass away. Everyone pays for it when you do.

## *Carrying*

When my daughter was very little, she had little interest in being carried around. She was content to toddle along on her own, exploring the world with her own two feet. Ironically, as she grew and her weight surpassed thirty pounds, she developed a sudden and intense desire to be held all the time. Oh, how convenient. And of course, being held is never enough. She wants to be carried long past the point where my arms feel like they might snap off, all while she wiggles, jumps, and plays in my grasp, completely oblivious to the toll it takes on my body.

Her lack of awareness is understandable—she is just a child, still learning about the world and her place in it. She doesn't yet grasp the concept of her own weight, how it affects those around her, or the strain it can put on those who love her. But this lack of awareness isn't exclusive to children. It seems there are plenty of adults who have also missed the memo that they are not feather-light, that they carry a weight that others can feel.

Beware of a person who believes they are weightless, for you will find yourself with buckling knees, straining to hold them up as they continue to play in your arms. We all carry weight—emotional, mental, or physical—and we all have the potential to be heavy for someone else. Recognizing your own weight, developing the strength to carry it yourself, and understanding the strain it can put on another is one of the most valuable gifts we can offer in our relationships.

This is a lesson I want my little one to learn sooner rather than later. We share these moments—her nestled in my arms, me carrying her down the hallway or through the park—but I know there must be a balance. When my arms start to ache and my back starts to protest, I gently set her down and say, "Time to use those strong legs Mommy made you." It's a small nudge toward independence, a reminder that she, too, has the power and strength to stand on her own. In these moments, I hope to teach her a lesson that will serve her for a lifetime: to understand her own weight, to respect the strength of others, and to know when to carry herself.

## *Savor*

If I have a handful of chocolate in my right hand and I offer some to Dahlia with my left, can you guess where her eyes are fixated the entire time? You guessed it—they are laser-focused on the right hand, the hand still brimming with chocolate. She's stuffing the chocolates from my left hand into her mouth as quickly as possible, her little cheeks puffed out like a chipmunk. As soon as she can swallow, she does, never pausing to savor the taste. The first thing she will say *once she can squeeze some air through her congested mouth* will be a request for what's in my right hand. Her desire is relentless, insatiable—always looking to the next thing, always wanting more.

It's amusing, yes, but also oddly revealing. Watching her, I can't help but see a reflection of a broader truth about human nature. As adults, how many of us are doing the same thing? We're so focused on what we want next that we rarely take a moment to truly savor what we already have. We chase after the metaphorical chocolates in someone else's hand, believing the next handful will finally be enough to satisfy us. Yet, in doing so, we overlook the sweetness of what's already in our grasp, what we once desired and now possess.

This simple moment with Dahlia is a reminder to myself, and perhaps to anyone reading this, of how easily we fall into the trap of constant wanting. We live in a culture that is perpetually focused on the next big thing—whether it's the next promotion, the next purchase, or the next big life milestone. We become so fixated on what's just out of reach that we forget to appreciate what's already in our grasp.

So, as I watch Dahlia's eyes dart back to my right hand, I take a moment to consider the lesson buried in her innocent greed.

It's a call to slow down and enjoy what we have before immediately seeking more. It's a reminder to savor the moment, to taste the chocolate, and to let the sweetness linger on our tongues a little longer. Because if we don't, we risk spending our lives in constant dissatisfaction, always reaching for more and never feeling fulfilled.

## *Play*

When we were kids, my mother always asked us, "When will you take life seriously?" She'd constantly remind us that life wasn't a game and that we needed to wake up to reality. At the time, her words felt like they came from another planet. We couldn't make sense of what she was saying. We were too busy being kids, thoughtlessly making a good time of everything we did. Spending even a moment in any other mindset just didn't add up. Life was a series of adventures to be explored, games to be played, and laughter to be had. Seriousness seemed like a foreign concept meant for adults—a distant future we couldn't fathom.

Now, as I watch my own child treat the world like a sprawling playground, I find myself struggling to find joy or fun in almost anything. It's as if the endless to-do lists, responsibilities, and pressures have stripped away that innate ability to find delight in the mundane. Yet, sometimes, I pay special attention to her, watching closely to see if she can extract fun from tasks that seem devoid of it. She might be picking up toys, sorting through laundry, or stirring a pot of pretend soup, but there is always a sparkle of play in her eyes, a giggle on her lips. And, of course, she is always successful in turning the most mundane moments into pure joy. I am left standing there, amazed and bewildered. I wonder how she does it. How does she take a world filled with routine and make it vibrant again?

Sometimes, I catch myself wanting her to grow up, just as my mother wanted for me. I find myself overstimulated by the constant play, the unending silliness, and the relentless noise that seems to have no off switch. There are days when my nerves feel frayed, stretched thin by the never-ending soundtrack of childhood. But I resist. I resist the urge to say or do anything that might take away her superpower—this magical ability to turn the mundane into play and accept nothing less. Somewhere along the way to becoming an adult, so many of us lost this superpower. We traded it for seriousness, efficiency, and "getting things done." We traded it for reality.

And I see now that this is a big reason why we struggle so much in raising a child. It's not just the sleepless nights, the messes that seem to regenerate, or the endless questions that fray our patience—it's that we've forgotten how to see the world through their eyes. We've lost the ability to find wonder in the everyday. To a child, the world is still full of magic. Every stick can be a sword, every puddle a portal, every moment an opportunity for adventure. They haven't yet been burdened by the weight of "taking life seriously."

The more we can turn the experience of parenting into play, the better it will be—for us and for our children. The more we embrace the spontaneity, the silliness, and the curiosity, the more our children will enjoy being around us. When we allow ourselves to play alongside them, we're not just entertaining them; we're reconnecting with a part of ourselves buried under adulthood's debris. In doing so, we might just rediscover that lost superpower within us—the ability to turn the ordinary into extraordinary, to transform the routine into something magical.

So now, I try to remind myself that life doesn't have to be as serious as I once believed it to be. Yes, there are responsibilities, bills to pay, and realities that must be faced. But there is also room for play, for wonder, for joy. There is room for us to meet our children where they are—in a world where everything can be a game, where the mundane can be magical, and where growing up doesn't mean losing the ability to see life as one great, big playground.

# About the Author

J.L.Ford is a writer, public speaker, educator and father. His work on culture, relationships, self-help and spiritual growth have been enjoyed by millions of people across the globe.

You can follow J.L. on instagram @authorjl and join him on Facebook at www.facebook.com/theauthorjl.

www.whatshetaughtmebook.com

www.ingramcontent.com/pod-product-compliance
Lightning Source LLC
Chambersburg PA
CBHW040314170426
43195CB00021B/2972